DOLLS

OF THE

TUSAYAN INDIANS

BY

J. WALTER FEWKES,

Copyright © 2013 Read Books Ltd.
This book is copyright and may not be
reproduced or copied in any way without
the express permission of the publisher in writing

British Library Cataloguing-in-Publication Data
A catalogue record for this book is available from the
British Library

Dolls

A doll is a model of a human being, often used as a toy for children. Dolls have traditionally been used in magic and religious rituals throughout the world, and dolls made of materials like clay and wood have been found in the Americas, Asia, Africa and Europe. The earliest documented dolls go back to the ancient civilizations of Egypt, Greece and Rome. Such dolls – specifically used as toys for girls, with moveable limbs and clothing, were notably documented in ancient Greece, created both as rudimentary playthings, but also as elaborate art. Today's doll manufacturing has its roots in Germany though, dating back to the fifteenth century. With industrialisation and the appearance of new materials like porcelain and plastic, dolls were increasingly mass-produced, and from this point onwards, right until the present day, dolls have become increasingly popular as simple toys and expensive collectibles.

The earliest dolls were made from available materials like clay, stone, wood, bone, ivory, leather and wax. Archaeological evidence places dolls as the foremost candidate for the world's oldest toy! Wooden paddle dolls (a type of female figurine found in burials) have been discovered in Egyptian tombs which date to as early as 2000 BCE. Dolls with movable appendages and removable outfits date back to at least 200 BCE. Greek dolls were made of clay and articulated at the hips and shoulders, and there are clear stories, dating from around

100 AD that describe such dolls being used by little girls as playthings. The modern dolls predecessors, the German models, have been documented as far back as the thirteenth century, with wooden dolls dating from the fifteenth century. From this point onwards, increasingly elaborate dolls were made for Nativity scenes, especially in Italy, and dolls with detailed, fashionable clothes were sold in France from the sixteenth century.

The German and Dutch 'peg wooden dolls' (using a jointing technique where the arms and/or legs are attached to the body with pegs), were cheap and simply made and were popular toys for poorer children in Europe. Wood continued to be the dominant material for doll construction until the nineteenth century, when it became increasingly combined with other materials such as leather, wax and porcelain. This allowed for doll construction to be far more intricate. It is unknown when dolls' glass eyes first appeared, but brown was the dominant eye colour for dolls up until the Victorian era when blue eyes became more popular, inspired by Queen Victoria. Interestingly, up until the middle of the nineteenth century, European dolls were predominantly made to represent grown-ups. Childlike dolls and the later ubiquitous baby doll did not appear until the 1850s, but by the late century, childlike dolls had overtaken the market.

The earliest celebrity dolls were 'Paper dolls'; dolls usually made of cardboard like materials, with separate clothes usually held onto the dolls by folding tabs. The nineteenth century ballerina paper dolls were among the earliest celebrity dolls, and the 1930s Shirley Temple doll sold in the millions, becoming one of the most successful celebrity dolls. A similar genre of doll, 'fashion dolls', were primarily designed to be dressed, and reflect fashion trends – usually modelled after teenage girls or adult women. Contemporary fashion dolls are typically made of vinyl, the most famous example of which, is the 'Barbie doll'. Barbies were made from 1959 onwards, by the American toy company Mattel, and have dominated the market from their inception. The only doll to challenge Barbie's dominance was the 'Bratz' make, reaching forty percent of the market share in 2006.

Despite their construction for children, some dolls, such as the nineteenth century bisque dolls, made by French manufacturers such as Bru and Jumeau, may be worth over £22,000 today. Dolls have also made it into the political and artistic spheres, with artists such as Hans Bellmer, who made surrealistic dolls with interchangeable limbs in the 1930s and 1940s, in opposition to the Nazi party's idolisation of the perfect Aryan body. East Village artist Greer Lankton became famous in the 1980s for her theatrical window displays of drug addicted, anorexic and mutant dolls, reflecting the deteriorating social conditions of America's 'cultural capital.' Many books (mostly aimed at children) have also dealt with dolls, for example tales such as *Whilhelmina. The Adventures of a Dutch Doll,* by Nora Pitt-Taylor and the *Raggedy Ann* books by Johnny

Gruelle, first published in 1918. Our fascination with dolls is showing no signs of waning in the present day, and it is hoped that the reader enjoys this book.

Separat-Abdruck aus: „Internationales Archiv für Ethnographie", Bd. VII. 1894.

DOLLS OF THE TUSAYAN INDIANS

BY

J. WALTER FEWKES,

BOSTON, MASS.

(With plates V–XI).

I have already elsewhere (*The American Anthropologist*, Jan. 1892) considered the simplest means used by these people in the expression of symbolism, that of their pictographs or rock etchings. In a natural sequence of subjects it might have been better to have followed this with an account of the symbolism expressed by them in the decoration of tiles, pottery, basket-ware and other productions, but at present this is not possible. In the glyptic art the Tusayan-Indians have a much more complicated means of expression and as a consequence their work of this kind is more elaborate and artistic. A commensurate description of their wood carving would be so large that I can not hope to give more than the barest outline of my subject, so that the present article [1]) must be regarded as more after the nature of a preliminary account. The specimens of wood carving to which especial attention will be given are dolls, *tí-hus* and fetishes, the latter introduced in secret performances. If we rely upon the testimony of the priests we may conclude that the art of wood carving among the *Hó-pi* (Mo-ki) is very ancient, and many of the objects placed on the altars in the subterranean chambers (*kib-vas*), where secret rites are performed, are said to have been brought up from the underworld when the ancients emerged from the *sí-pā-pu.* [2]) The majority of the specimens of wood carving which are here described are very modern. The objects treated in this article are called *tí-hus*, and are used by children as dolls.

These carved wooden images are made in great numbers by the Tusayan Indians and present most instructive objects for the study of symbolic decoration. They are interesting as affording valuable information in regard to the *Hó-pi* conception of their mythological personages.

These images are commonly mentioned by American visitors to the Tusayan pueblos as idols, but there is abundant evidence to show that they are at present used simply as children's playthings which are made for that purpose and given to the girls with that thought in mind. [3])

---

[1]) The material which has served as a basis for the present article was collected in Wál-pi in the summers of 1891, '92, while attached to the Hemenway Southwestern Archaeological Expedition. Many of the specimens were purchased from their owners, and from these and notes, drawings, and photographs of others not obtained, the accompanying descriptions were written. There were a few which I have seen, in which the details of symbolism somewhat differ from those described, but I have endeavored to mention the more salient points of their symbolic decoration.

The majority of these dolls were exhibited in the „Historico-Americana Exposicion en Madrid".

[2]) The traditional opening in the earth, out of which the races of man originally emerged. (See *Journal of American Ethnology and Archaeology*, Vol. II). A similar name is used by other writers as that of a lake associated with the origin and final destiny of pueblo peoples.

[3]) I have not yet observed any ceremony of consecration, but such may exist.

These figurines are generally made by participants in the *Ni-mán-kā-tci-nā* [1]) and are presented to the children in July or August at the time of the celebration of the farewell of the *Ka-tci-nas*. It is not rare to see the little girls after the presentation carrying the dolls about on their backs wrapped in their blankets in the same manner in which babies are carried by their mothers or sisters. Those dolls which are more elaborately made are generally hung up as ornaments in the rooms, but never, as far as I have investigated the subject, are they worshipped. The readiness with which they are sold for a proper remuneration shows that they are not regarded as objects of reverence.

As so commonly happens in instances of carving, either in stone or wood, among many primitive peoples, there is a great similarity in general form with an indication by the symbolic markings, of the special personage intended. They have a conventionalized human form which is adhered to throughout, but the special or individual character intended to be represented is indicated by appropriate symbolism in the accompanying markings. The same is true, in the productions of figurines by other primitive people. A sign, a mark, a small appendage, is used to denote personality and with these exceptions there is a general similarity throughout them all. It is only when we come to higher stages of culture that an attempt is made in glyptic representations to delineate by expression the characters which are associated with mythological personages. The *tí-hus* are generally images of deities or mythological personages, and these Indians have not progressed out of that stage of culture in which the mind resorts to an elaborate symbolism to convey its conceptions. They have not advanced to that culture in which benificent or malignant characteristics can be expressed by facial expression, consequently the most important thing to study in these carvings, is the symbolism, and it will be found that every ornamentation of this kind has its special significance. Moreover that symbolism is widely spread and is not confined to these *tí-hus*, but is identical in meaning wherever it occurs, whether on pottery, basket ware, blankets or the adornment of paraphernalia used in religious ceremonials. As among other peoples conventionalised markings may be combined with realistic representations to explain characters of figures in bas-relief, or to record the history of distinguished personages, so symbolistic markings on the bodies and faces of these *tí-hus* indicate their identities, thus becoming perfect ideographic modes of expression.

The carving of these dolls is executed in that true archaic fashion, which is seen in the dawn of art among all people. The representation of the body is subordinate to that of the head, often appearing as a shapeless imitation, but more generally as a conventionalized figure, so that there is little to distinguish the different *Kā-tci-nās* [2]) which are represented, by the forms of their bodies. No attempt was made to imitate muscles or to delineate the details of the anatomy. The highest differentiation was made in the decoration

---

[1]) The spelling of Tusayan words is essentially that adopted in my article on the summer ceremonials (*Journal of American Ethnology and Archaëology* Vol. II. N°. 1): *a* = *a* in father; *e* = *e* in whey; *i* = *e* in me; *o* = *ō*, note; *ü* = French *u*, tu; *ñ* = *ng*. The sounds of *b* and *p* are not differentiated. It is also difficult to distinguish *d* and *t* sounds (*dá-wa* or *tá-wa*). Different observers detect one sound or the other and legitimately give different spelling according to the sound heard. *c* = *sh* in show. *s* has sometimes a slight *sh* sound as in *Sa-li-ko* or *S(h)a-li-ko*; *v* = *kv.*; *kc* like *ch* in chink. Other letters as in English. The many ways of spelling aboriginal words, adopted by different authors, makes this portion of my article unsatisfactory. The praiseworthy efforts of the Bureau of Ethnology, to definately determine the letters for different sounds, can make little headway as long as different members of the institution adopt different sounds for the same letter. For a description of the *Ni-man-ka-tci-na* see Journal of American Ethnology and Archaëology, Vol. II. N°. 1.

[2]) Supernatural intercessors between men and gods. (See *Journal* of *American Ethnology* Vol. II.)

of the same with paint, but in this respect certain established conventional patterns were followed and these are not definite enough to distinguish the *Ka-tci-nas*. The characteristic details were always found on the head. The mask or helmet with its symbolic decorations was made to express characteristics of the *Ka-tci-nas* and care was given to delineate upon this part of the doll those features, or symbolic markings, by which they were distinguished.

It is on that account that the study of pictographs, which are limited generally to representations of the head, has an importance in the study of mythology. Hence it is also that the faces of the dolls are most carefully decorated, and that the most important details of carving are found upon them. Most careful attention to the coloration is also universal. If the different figures be examined it will be found that the head of one doll might equally well be found upon the body of another, but when such a change is made although the bodies of the two are the same, the character of the doll is changed. The symbolism is best expressed on the heads of the *tí-hus*.

On Egyptian statues we find something similar. It is to the heads of these that one looks for the characters of the god represented. According to Westropp "gods and goddesses were principally distinguished according to their head-dresses." This applies equally well to the figurines of other peoples, and indicates an archaic form of representation which belongs to the youth of most, if not all races. This fact is one which gives a great importance to the study of helmets, masks and all cephalic decorations which are used in ceremonial dances.

The colors used in painting or in staining the figurines are obtained in various ways, and are either mineral or vegetable. The five colors: yellow, green, red, black, and white, which are generally used can all be obtained from the soil. Their dark reds, which are used in the decoration of the body, are pulverized specular iron and ochres, generally applied to the body, with the hands moistened with saliva. A variety of reds ranging from pink to scarlet are obtained from sumach berries and other vegetable substances.

Where green is used it is commonly made from malachite or some copper carbonate. Pounded shale, thin strata of which underlie the mesa, and corn-smut furnish fine black pigments, and kaolin of various degrees of purity is used for white. In addition to these native colors at the present day the well known aniline dyes [1]) are very commonly employed. When the paint is applied to the doll it is not "fixed" in any way and is often very easily rubbed off so that great care must be taken in handling the objects to preserve their colors.

---

[1]) Colors purchased from American traders are fast driving out the native pigments in all articles of Tusayan handiwork. From an Ethnological standpoint this is much to be regretted, but the ease with which they can be used, favours their adoption. It is rare to find articles manufactured at the present day which do not show the introduced colors. On the painting of prayerofferings or sticks, called *pá-hos*, however the old pigments are still almost universally retained.

In the mechanical work of carving wood the knife is generally used, but a stone is sometimes employed to grind down and smooth flat portions of the object. The older images used in ceremonies were probably all made with stone implements. The wood employed is a very light and soft root-branch of the cottonwood-tree. In cutting the wood the image is held in the palm of the hand, pressed against the body as a support, and the knife drawn towards the same. Polishing is ordinarily done with a smooth stone.

In the construction of wooden *pá-hos*, where the carving is less elaborate, all the work is done with stone with the exception of cutting off the *pá-hos* the proper length. When the *pá-ho* is sharpened, it is held in the palm of the hand, the point turned to the wrist and the knife is drawn towards the arm.

A Yucca-stick with the end chewed into a brush, is used in painting lines. Plane surfaces of the doll are painted by squirting on the color from the mouth. This latter method is an almost universal one, in the painting of dance objects. Camel's hair brushes have not yet come into use.

The dolls which we are to consider, are either imitations of figurines used in ceremonials or traditional forms universally recognized.

In studying the specimens of wood carving it will be noticed that some of the more important personages in the mythology of the Indians are not represented, and there are several of these wooden images which are introduced in the ceremonials, and are more or less venerated. There is every evidence to believe that these are much more ancient than the dolls, and it is commonly reported that many of them have a great antiquity.

The majority of the wooden images, which are introduced in ceremonials, are without legs and bear the simplest symbolic decorations. They are commonly placed before the altars, set in piles of sand and are sprinkled with sacred meal during the ceremonies. This usage recalls what is reported by the early writers in describing the Caribs of the West-Indies, who had a similar custom of sprinkling their stone images called *Zemes.* A consideration of the various figurines which are introduced in the secret ceremonials among the Tusayan Indians would swell this account to undue proportions, and I have thought it better to reserve descriptions of them for my accounts of the ceremonies [1]) in which they occur, but a brief mention of one or two may well be inserted here.

In my account [2]) of the *Lá-la-kon-ti*, which is celebrated in the September-moon, I have described four of these wooden figures which are placed before the altar. It is an interesting fact that of these four, three have the chin painted black. When we remember that in many ceremonials this characteristic painting of the face is found, it leads us to inquire why it has not some meaning. We may interpret this as an archaic feature among the images of these Indians. It is certainly significant as being so common a character on ancient idols. [3]) In the celebration of the ceremony of the December-moon, there is introduced a figure of the head of the great serpent, *Ba-lü-lü-koñ*, which by a skillfully arranged mechanism is made to appear to speak, a priest being concealed behind an artificial screen.

A somewhat similar contrivance which has already been described among the Vancouver-Island Indians and has been recorded in the ceremonials of the Caribs, was not unknown in classical times, and is a most interesting instance of the carrying out of a similar idea among widely different peoples. The fact that these idols used in ceremonials are sprinkled with meal and adorned with feathers, would seem to indicate that a certain amount of reverence was attached to them, as images of the personage venerated. During certain rites they are carried in the hands of the celebrants, but, I cannot however believe that the worship is anything more than a reverence for their antiquity, not unlike a similar feeling which ancient images inspire among all people. Closely connected with the use of these wooden images employed in ceremonials is that of the various stone fetishes [4]), many examples of which are found in the villages. A consideration of these deserves a more appropriate place in a special paper on this subject, but it seems well to casually mention certain groups of them which one finds. The smallest of these, often worn as charms or carried as hunting stones for various purposes, are seldom seen, but can be

---

[1]) *Journal* of *American Ethnology and Archaëology.* Vol. II N⁰. 1.

[2]) See: The *Lá-la-kon-ti*, *American Anthropologist.* April, 1892.

[3]) Seo also figures in various Central American Codices (*Codex Cortesianus*), in which portions of the face and chin are differently colored.

[4]) The reader must not expect to find a description of the symbolism of all the supernatural beings which figure in the Tusayan pantheon. The article deals principally with those, that are used as dolls.

collected with little difficulty. In many of the houses there are large stone images standing in conspicuous places. IN-TI-WA, *A Hó-pi* priest, has a stone image of *Pü-ü-koñ*, the war-god, two or three feet tall, which is one of the best stone figurines in the village of Walpi. This example is made of an oblong black stone with no representation of the arms and legs. There is a slight constriction for the neck and markings to indicate the eyes, and two rude scratches are found on either cheek. Around the neck are tied many feathers which from time to time are abundantly sprinkled with meal. The idol stands in a conspicuous place near the middle of the room on one side and is regarded with great reverence by the family.

A fetish of the mountain-lion is to be seen in a house in the pueblo, Ha-no. This specimen is somewhat more artistically cut than that of the war-god and is about eight inches long. Around its neck are tied breath feathers [1]) and piñon needles. I have studied several other specimens of these stone idols and believe they are not uncommon throughout the villages. To this category probably belongs the well graven, squatting figure of a human being, at present on exhibition in the National Museum, Washington, which figure however was made by a man [2]) yet living (1892).

Botryoidal stones of strange shape with no semblance to an animal or human form are found in many shrines. One of the most interesting of these is in the shrine which is situated at a place in the East mesa called Wal-la, the gap. This is simply a natural coiled fragment. In a niche in the Snake-rock there is a shapeless stone, the ancient *Hē-hé-a*, which is also regarded with sanctity by the people. The fetishes which are introduced on the altar of the Antelopes in the Snake-dance will be considered in my monograph on that ceremony, and in a later publication I hope to bring together other forms of these stone idols which I have observed in the Tusayan villages.

It is extremely difficult in the study of the religions of primitive peoples to draw a sharp line of demarcation between pure idols, which are worshipped and those figures of the same, which have a purely secular character. It can hardly be said that these dolls are worshipped at the present day. Still it by no means follows that they may not be copies of images which have been worshipped, although they now have come to have a strictly secular use. The corresponding images which appear in sacred ceremonials no doubt have a sacred character from their antiquity, but we can hardly declare that even these images are worshipped. We may rather say that they are reverenced for their age. Symbolic figures of all kinds as representatives of something more than purely secular objects, but if similar figures were ever worshipped, at the present day they have lost their character. The resemblances between the words idol and doll are significant. I believe the Tusayan Indians regard these dolls as purely secular in the same way for instance, that they regard pictographs, and that there is no feeling of veneration connected in their minds with these images carved out of wood. With the stone images and fetishes it may be different. A somewhat similar condition is seen in the Zemes of the West Indian Islands [3]), as has been elsewhere shown.

---

1) Feathers from the breast of the eagle below the wings.

2) HÓ-NA-NI (bear) a Tewan, whose home is in Keam's Cañon.

3) The inhabitants of Easter Island may have looked upon the carefully carved wooden images which are known from those islands, in the same light as the Ho-pi regarded their wood carving. It is not wholly clear, however, that they were regarded as dolls. The skill with which these islanders carved wood is beautifully shown in specimens now preserved in the Museum of the Peabody Academy of Science

I was kindly allowed by Prof. O. T. MASON, to whom my thanks are due for this and other kindnesses, to examine the collection of Tusayan and Zuñi dolls of the Bureau of Ethnology in the National Museum at Washington. This collection which contains many examples of wood carving, was collected by Maj. POWELL and Col. STEVENSON, and as it contains many duplicates, is a most interesting one for comparative study. The majority of these I have been able to identify, using as types the specimens which had been named for me by the Indians themselves. The specimens on exhibition in the Museum have been carefully repainted and the remainder of the collection is in much the same condition as when brought from the Southwest. The latter are very instructive to study, although the localities from which they were collected are not clearly stated.

In looking over this collection, I have been struck with the variety of decoration which the duplicates show, and I am led to believe that great care must be used in defining the symbolism from any one specimen. The majority are made of cottonwood, although three are carved out of other kinds of wood, but as the latter are unfinished, they are not of value for this article.

A-hül-ka-tci-na.

In the Washington collection of *tí-hus* there is a figurine of *A-hül-ka-tcí-na* which has been indentified from a colored sketch, submitted to the inspection of several of the Indians. This *ka-tcí-na* is said to appear in the ceremony called *Po-wúm-ûh*. The right side of the face is painted green; the left black. On the forehead of the green side there are black, and on the forehead of the left or black side, white crosses. The position of the mouth is occupied by a triangular black figure with an elongated bar of yellow; the face is bordered with white. A strip of thin leather, dentated on the edges, surrounds the head. This personage is said to he the eldest brother of *Tú-mac* and their father is *Tuñ-wúb.* [1]) I have been told by Mr. STEPHEN, that in the *Po-wúm-ûh* ceremony he goes to the houses of all who have a chieftains badge (*tí-po-ni*). [2]) that is to all who are chiefs, priests or priestesses, and marks the side of the doorway with prayer meal. As he does this, he utters the word „*á-hu*" four times, beginning with a deep base, changing to a high falsetto and continuing it as long as he has breath. I have a doll of *Ai'-wo-to-to*, a personage who plays a prominent part in the ceremony of the morning following the Ni-man, as been described, but it adds nothing to my account (See: Journal, Vol. II. N°. 1.)

While I was engaged in the study of the ornamentation of the masks, several helmets bearing decorations from previous ceremonials, were brought in to be repainted. One of these was ornamented in a most characteristic fashion. For it was given the name *A-ho-te-ka-tci-na.* It was painted yellow and bore upon its face a number of four-pointed stars, the colors of which varied in different figures. In the middle of the mask between the eyes

---

at Salem, and other specimens of a similar character are figured by several Ethnologists. A special paper might be devoted to a description of the Salem specimens and a comparative study with those figured by RATZEL, THOMPSON, and other observers (PARTINGTON). Among the most instructive are ten in the STURGIS-Collection, in the American Museum of Natural History in New-York City. Many figurines illustrating this condition were exhibited in the Historical Exposition in Madrid.

[1]) See: Ceremony of the *Ni-mán-ka-tci-na.* A Journal of *American Ethnology and Archaeology* Vol. II.

[2]) The *ti-po-ni*, as I have already explained, is the palladium of the priesthood or society. This so called "mother" figures in most of the ceremonials and is a badge of the priesthood. See descriptions of *Lá-la-kon-ti Man-zráu-ti*, etc. etc. The snake- and Antelope-fraternities each has its own *ti-po-ni* which figures conspicuously, as I shall show, in secret observances.

was a black star, on the left of which was a red and on the right a green. Above the latter was a white star and above the former a green.

In the middle of the forehead there was a star with one point painted red, another green, and the two remaining points speckled white and black. On the left of the mouth was a green star, and on the right a black. Around the upper margin of the helmet dried plant fibres were tied, and on the lower rim a small cloth. This interesting mask I have never seen worn, and I am not able to tell in what dance it appears. The men insisted that it was the mask of *A-hó-te-ka-tci-na.*

A-hó-te-ka-tcí-na.

A *tí-hu* of *A-hó-te* is one of the simple dolls which have been observed. The head is black with two lateral horns, girt with green and black bands. Upon the forehead there is a triangular area bordered with green, along the outer rim of which are round green spots. The green band of the forehead has a red zone within, while the enclosed area is yellow with round spots of white, black, and red. To the top of the head is tied a bunch of feathers.

Upon the right cheek there is a six-pointed star, on the left two crescents with horns turned in opposite ways. The neck and left arm are yellow; the left forearm green. The right arm is green, the forearm yellow. A black band girts the inner border of the arm and extends across the breast. The body is white, crossed by longitudinal red lines, one of which is median, the others extending to the knees. There are black garters about the knees. The left leg is green, the right yellow; the sides of the feet and the soles of the same are red. A sprig of cedar surrounds the neck.

A-vatc-ka-tci-na. Pl. IX Fig. 29.[1])

A doll of *A-vatc* has a black face, upon the medial line of which there is a zigzag line of blue bordered with red. The eyes are red with black pupils, surrounded by a circle of green spots, and the mouth is prolonged into a cylindrical snout. Upon the right side of the head there is a conventionalized flower (squash) symbol, and upon the left two long upright feathers and stiff horsehair, stained red. A bundle of feathers, stained yellow and green, is tied to the back of the head. The doll has a round cylindrical snout, the tip of which is painted red. A figure of the frog is painted on the back of the head. The hips are much enlarged and the body is bright red; the right arm is yellow, the forearm green, and the left arm green, the forearm yellow. The left leg is green, the right yellow. The feet are red.

Bá-lü-lü-koñ.

The mythical plumed-serpent I have seen represented in pictographs. He is also depicted on the kilts of the snake priests and a figurine of his head arranged in the middle of a bower of artificial flowers was observed by Mr. Stephen, in the dances at the winter solstice. The head of this snake bears a horn and a crest of feathers. A drop of water is represented as hanging from the mouth, and along the sides of the body there are

---

[1]) The text is not necessarily a description of the representative doll figured. Consequently when there is a variation between the two it implies a description of one doll and a figure of another of the same divinity.

represented alternating parallel marks[1]) and arrow heads. I have not seen a doll of this divinity.

A figurine of *Bá-lü-lü-koñ* is introduced in a winter ceremonial, in which it is skillfully thrust through openings in an altar, covered with a swinging lappet on which is depicted a figure of the sun. This ceremony and the altar will be described later. In the collection of the Bureau of Ethnology there is a *tí-hu* of a Snake Priest, *Tcu-a-wymp-kia*, with symbols of *Ba-lü-lü-koñ* on the dance kilt.

Ka-vá-ho-ka-tci-na.

The word *ka-vá-ho* is evidently from the Spanish *Cavallo*, horse, and gives the name to a *Ka-tci-na* who bears the figure of a horse upon his cheek. I have seen this *Ka-tcí-na* several times and have spoken of him in my description of the summer ceremonials of the Tusayan Indians (Journal Vol. II.) The bear-*Ka-tcí-na* or *Ho-nán-i* is designated by the marks of the bears foot upon the cheek. I have seen a doll of the bear-*Ka-tcí-na* and also have seen him personified in the dances. This *Ka-tcí-na* is very easily confounded with the badger, which has a similar symbol of a claw depicted on the cheek.

Cí-tü-tü (ka-tci-na).

The *tí-hu* of this *ka-tci-na?* has a rounded head, crossed by a number of vertical lines of different color. The medial line is black and on either side there are colored lines in the following order: yellow, black, red, black, white, black, and green. One of these black lines is broken by white marks. *Cí-tü-tü* wears a blanket and has painted on it a ceremonial sash, but the colors were too much obliterated for me to make them out. This doll was observed in *Wál-pi*, but I have not been able to purchase it.

I have seen the helmet of *Ci-tü-tü* which is similarly colored to the head of the *ti-hu.*

Co-tük-i-nuñ-wû. Pl. XI Fig. 39.

A doll of the star-god is readily recognized by the star symbol, a four-pointed star which is shown upon the face. The head of this doll has also a star symbol in the form of a horizontal cross, made of two sticks. The body is brown and yellow and the head is black with white stars. The symbol of the Star-god which is common on shields is a cross with arms of equal length.

The doll figured (Fig. 39) has a single curved appendage on the top of the head. This is quite common in pictographs of shields on which the star-god symbol in often found.

Du-mâs-ka-tci-na. Pl. XI Fig. 41.

I have collected a specimen of a doll for which this name has been given me. Upon each side of the head it bears a thin wooden slab or terraced tablet. The position of the mouth is occupied by a triangular black figure recalling similar figures on women's blankets. A somewhat similar doll has the same formed appendages at the sides of the head with figures of the raincloud upon them. To this the name of *O-mow-ûh* has been given.

One of the most interesting dolls in the collection likewise has the triangular mouth

---

1) The attention of the reader is called to similar marks on the plumed serpent figured in the *Codex Cortesianus*, the original of which is in Madrid. I am inclined to believe that these marks are feather symbols.

of *Dú-mas*[1]) but stretched over the top of the head is a figure painted in three colors, red, yellow, and green. Around the top of the head there is nailed a piece of leather upon which are cloud symbols with falling rain, and above these zigzag sticks to which are given the name of lightning sticks are inserted. I do not know the name of this doll but some of the Indians have pointed to the lightning stick and called it the lightning *kā-tci-nā*. Its face is painted green, and the figure carried on the head was made to indicate a rainbow, if we judge from the parallel bands and white markings.

Gai-tó-ya.

This personage is a great reptile but not *Bá-lü-lü-koñ*, the great plumed snake. He is said to exist in the far off mountains at the present time and a similar conception occurs among the other pueblos and also among the Navajos. In the Snake legend he is represented as guarding the *Sí-pa-pû*. His body is described as not longer than the arm and as thick as a man's body. The eyes are very large and its great teeth can pierce the thickest skin. The body is gray, but its head is all colors, and by its breath it can cause death at a distance. This snake is regarded as the guardian of all snakes. I have never seen a figurine of him and am not familiar with any representation.

Hā-hai-wüq-ti. Pl. IX Fig. 27.

The doll which I have of *Hā-hai-wüq-ti* is a little over seven inches in length and over three inches in diameter. It represents a stout old woman, and has the characteristic face of the mark of the mother of *nā-tác-kā*, which is later described.

The top and back of the head is painted black leaving a semicircular white face. There are two ear-like cephalic appendages of a red color. A cluster of feathers is tied to the crown of the head. The white face is crossed by vertical red lines. In the middle of each cheek there is a round red spot. The eyes and mouth are indicated by black crescents curved upwards, placed below round black spots. In front of the ears there hangs down to the neck on each side a coil of black yarn representing hair and imparting a characteristic appearance to the *ti-hu*. These are the matron symbols and are characteristic of the way the married women dress their hair in Há-no.

The blanket carved in the wood is white, girt on either border with broad and narrow parallel red lines and surrounded on the rim and down the front with a blue border. The V-shaped portion of the dress showing beneath the blanket in front is black, and a girdle of red, yellow, and black is painted about the waist. The lower border of the garment is blue and yellow. The legs are white with a black rim about the borders of the feet.

Hák-a-to. Pl. V Fig. 3.

In the collection of dolls which I have made, there is one for which the above name has been given. It is distinguished by a round white wooden bar on the top of the head, projecting a short distance on either side. To the ends of this bar are tied short woolen

---

1) The father? of this person *Tuñ-wub* is represented on the altar in the more elaborate secret rites connected with the *Ni-man* (Farewell) *Ka-tci-na* dance. Although I have never seen a figurine of the father, the figures on the altars convey a very good idea of the symbolism. He bears a crest of feathers represented by marks above his head, two horns, and an arrow point on the forehead. In the figure this person bears a branch of some kind in each hand.

filaments. The marks upon the face are several parallel lines extending vertically on each side of the eyes. It is said that this is a Zuñi-*ka-tci-na*, and has been imitated by the Tusayan people.

Hó-chan-ĕ. Pl. VII Fig. 17.

The doll of this person has the upper part of the face painted black with a red border. It has two large disk-shaped eyes raised from the surface of the face. The lower portion of the face is green, and the mouth has the form of a duck's-bill. A horizontal feather is placed through an opening in each ear and the hair is made of skin with the wool stained black. The body is red with two yellow lines on each shoulderblade. The lower legs are yellow and green, and the feet are red.

Hu-mis-ka-tci-na. Pl. V Fig. 1.

The *ti-hu* of the *Hu-mis-ka-tci-na* is one of the most elaborate which I have in my collection, and is one of the most successful examples of *Ho-pi*-woodcarving which I have seen. The cephalic tablet or *nāk-tci* has the terraced form and is made of a slab of wood half an inch thick, four and a half inches wide, and six inches high. The decorations upon it are similar to those on *nāk-tci* worn in the dance which is described elsewhere.[1])

The ground of the *nāk-tci* is painted green. Above the helmet there is a rainbow semicircle enclosing a green field in which is a black triangle with a transverse bar of white and black, with patches of white. The symbolic rainbow is made up of concentric semicircles of lines of the following colors from the smaller to the larger: black, red, black, brown and black. Five white marks are arranged at intervals in the black semicircle which separates the red from the brown. This rainbow symbol is capped by a variegated figure which fills most of the central part of the upper region of the *nāk-tci*. The two sides of this figure are formed of black bands which are continued into a rounded knot with white centre and black border. The lefthand zone of the figure is brown, the right red and they are separated by a black line with two white marks. They extend a short distance into the apical prolongation of the figure. The top of this apical prolongation is rounded with a black border and a white centre which is crossed by a black band.

On the level with the visor of the helmet there extends to the border of the *nak-tci* five bands of the following colors on either side: black, red, black, brown, and black. The middle black line is broken by a single white spot. These lines represent the continuation of the rainbow semicircles of the visor of the helmet and vertically from them there arises a broad black band tipped with a semicircle slightly broader than the band. This is white in the middle, lined with black and crossed by a black band. From the lower rim of the mask to the rim of the *nak-tci* there is a black band broken by transverse white lines. Upon this arises vertically a black band with a white rectangle near the middle of the upper end, and between it and the edge of the *nak-tci* is a double terraced red colored figure lined with black. The two terraces of each have white semicircles tipped with black. All the above figures are different conceptions of *O-mow-uh*-(cloud-) symbols and the whole *nak-tci* is an *O-mow-ûh*-sign[2]). (Pl. VI Fig. 11.)

---

[1]) *A Journal of American Ethnology and Archaeology.* Vol. II. N⁰. 1.
[2]) A somewhat similar headdress is found on the head of the Mexican Rain God.

From the angle of the two terraces at the rim of the *nak-tci* there arises a long sprig of seed grass and a small feather. The ornamentation of the reverse of the *nak-tci* is identical with that of the obverse.

The top of the head is painted white with the visor the same color. The under surface of the visor is red. A number of feathers extend at right angles from the upper rim of the visor hanging over it and the face. The face is divided by a median black band, marked with three white rings[1]), into two halves, one brown, the other or the right green. At the point of junction of the visor with the upper part of the face there is a band of white in which are painted in black four long *O-mow-uh*-symbols whose lower edges rest on a black line. The brown half of the face is bordered by a black line outside of which is a green, and the green half of the face is outlined by a similar black line with a red margin. On each side from the black border there extends for a short distance on the green and brown fields at the upper and lower ends a triangle in black. The eyes are represented by black slits extending almost across the fields and slightly enlarged nearest the medial line.

The lower border of the face is crossed by a broad black band ornamented with four white marks, and three sets of red, green, and brown marks. The underside, or chin below the helmet, and the back of the head, are painted white. From its middle line arises a red stick as long as the *nak-tci* from the tip of which extends a bundle of feathers. At its junction with the helmet there are also a bundle of feathers and a small hank of wool.

The body is painted black. The arms are separated from the body; the left extended by the side, the right raised originally holding a carved wooden rattle. Hanks of wool are tied about the wrists. A green band girts the upper arm on both sides. The legs are painted black and the feet red. A piece of woolen yarn is tied above the knee, and there is a black band above the red one on the ankles.

The *ti-hu* wears a white cotton blanket with a black border, over which is a broad sash with red, green, and white embroidered ends. Over this about the waist is tied a woven sash in imitation of the women's sashes. Piñon boughs are tied in the kilts, and a sprig of piñon surrounds the neck.

I have already elsewhere (*Journal of American Ethnology and Archaeology*, Vol. II. Nº. 1 plate) figured the doll of the socalled *Si-ó-hu-mis* or Zuñi *Hu-mis-ka-tci-na*, which is described in following pages of this work.

The *Hu-mis-ka-tci-na* is a corn *Ka-tci-na* or literally, according to Stephen, the one who makes corn grow high in far stretching rows with spreading waving tassels. His home is said to be *Kaio-yuba*, which is a spring to which a messenger is sent with an offering. The road through which blessings come to the shrine is represented in the ceremony by a cotton string and is extended in the direction of the spring so that blessings may come through it.

A carved specimen of the helmet and the surmounting tablet of the *Hu-mis-ka-tci-na* is on exhibition in the National Museum, at Washington. This resembles with little variation the helmet which I have already described.

---

[1]) Imprint of a reed or rush which grows near water. They are called *Poñ-o-ki-ya-tu*.

Há-ku-wûh.

One sometimes finds among the Tusayan Indians a doll which is immediately characterized by the legs crossed. The character represented in this way took part in the *Wá-wac* or Racing *Ka-tci-na* at Há-no and is one of many similar personages who appear in the presentation of this more or less secular event.

Hä-wüq-ti. Pl. VI Fig. 7.

I have a doll of this woman who is said to appear in the *Po-wúm-ûh.* The symbolism is very simple and hardly distinctly enough marked, to separate her form one or two others. The mouth and teeth, and the small long tuft of hair on the head are characteristic. *Soi-yo-kim-wüq-ti* and *Soi-yok-ma-na*, who are also said to appear in the *Po-wúm-ûh*, I have not been able to see.

Hē-hé-a-ka-tci-na. Pl. VII Fig. 16 & Pl. VIII Fig. 18.

The different forms of these dolls all agree in having four zigzag lightning marks on the face. These are placed vertically, two on the forehead and two on the cheeks, on each side. The nose and mouth are represented by a raised V-shaped body, painted red. In one specimen the lips are indicated by white spots. The color of the face, however, varies in different specimens [1]).

Tca-kwai-na. Pl. X Fig. 34.

The doll of this person has an oval face, painted black with mouth, furnished with teeth, surrounded by red lips. Out of this mouth there hangs a piece of leather, shaped like a spatula and colored bright red. This represents the tongue. From the middle of the chin, which is painted white, there hangs a cluster of long black horse hair. I have seen the mask of this person which is identical with that represented on the doll.

Ko-ho-ni-no-ka-tci-nā. Pl. VII Fig. 15.

A figurine of *Ko-ho-ni-no-ka-tci-nā* for the identification of which I am indebted to Mr. Stephen, has a shield-shaped face with a round spot on each cheek. On this spot is a ring of smaller dots. The eyes are narrow, black bands and the markings of the chin consist of parallel vertical marks. There are two spreading horns girt by different colored bands, red, yellow, green, and white.

The *ti-hu* represents a *ko-ho-ni-no*-dancer whom I have not seen personified in the

---

[1]) It is interesting to note, as possibly an instance of stalk and stone animism, that the botryoidal hematitic stone, said to be the original deity of this *Ka-tci-na*, is kept in the small crevice in the sacred rock. Instances which might be mentioned to illustrate stone worship are many, but in most cases I believe, it is not so much the image itself, as it is the age and the continued veneration in which the stone has been held which give it its sanctity.

As an instance of the readiness with which Indians endow stones with the powers of fetishes, may be mentioned the method adopted by them in the cure of sickness. When the shamans remove the cause of the trouble from the afflicted, they generally give one to understand that they take from the body a stone or an arrow point or some other foreign body which has caused the trouble. Those familiar with folklore among other tribes, will recognize the similarity of this custom among widely different people. The inner conception which has led to this belief is probably identical among all people who practise this method of cure, and is amply discussed in Tylor's Primitive Culture.

Tusayan ceremonials [1]). The cut represents a figure of this *Ka-tci-na* painted on a tile.

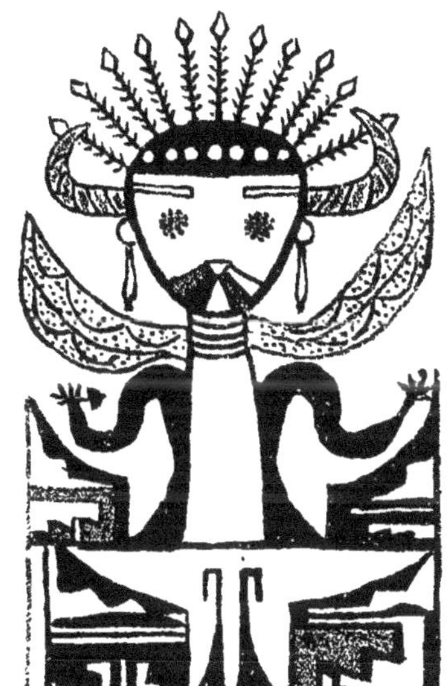

Ko-ho-ni-no Ka-tci-na
(depicted on tile).

Kók-le-ka-tcí-na.

There are several dolls of *Kok-lĕ*, the faces of which resemble the decorations so often seen in pottery. Upon each cheek there is an arrow-head, and the mouth has a crescentic line above it. Above the eyes are also crescentic lines with lateral branches on the convex side.

Ko-ko-pe'l-i.

This figurine is the representation of a personage whose characteristics are of a phallic nature. The face is black with a white median line which is continued down the back of the head. There is on each side of the head a white circle crossed by black lines at right angles to each other. The eyes are elongated slits, white with black centres. The hump on the back represents the bundle of food or presents which he bears as gifts for women.

There are several specimens of *Ko-ko-pĕ'l-i* in the Bureau of Ethnology collection at Washington, all of which have the symbolic characters well shown [2]). Figures of *Ko-ko-pĕ'l-i* can be seen on consultation with the author.

The black face with a median white line, a ring with two diameters on the side of the head, the hump back and a phallic feature which needs not be described here are found in all these examples. The four quadrants of the ring on the side of the head [3]) in one *Ko-ko-pĕ'l-i* are colored yellow, green, red, and white, following a circuit opposite the motion of the hands of a watch. These colors correspond with N, W, S, E, or the ceremonial circuit.

Kwa-hus-alek-to-ka. Pl. VII Fig. 12.

The eagle-tailed figurine has a green face with black eyes. The mouth is represented

---

[1]) A figure of this *Ka-tci-na* taken form a slab is introduced in the plates. (Pl. X Fig. 36). We know comparatively nothing of the ceremonies or the mythology of these Indians which fact imparts a great interest to this unique specimen. The Kohonino Indians form a small tribe, related to the Pueblos, but do not build houses. They dwell in and about the Grand Cañon of the Colorado and have more or less communication with the Hopi They have been visited and studied by STEPHEN, CUSHING and others and offer a most interesting problem, either in arrested pueblo development or degeneration. Their true relationships are yet to be made out as very little is known of their folk-lore, language, ceremonials or customs.

[2]) I have examined specimens of ladles, the handles of which are made in imitation of *Ta-tcúk-ti*, *Ko-ko-pĕ'l-i* and different *Ka-tci-nas*. The two former may be readily recognized, by comparisons with my figúres of the *ti-hus*.

[3]) A helmet which I have observed in one of the kib-vas, has a decoration on each side which resembles very closely similar decorations. On each side of the head, which was painted black, there was a circle with five sectors. The radii of these divisions were drawn in black. The upper part was green, the right yellow, the lower one of the left speckled, and the left red. Segments were drawn in the periphery of these sectors which were colored as follows. Red was depicted in the green, green in the yellow, red and yellow in the speckled. and white in the red. The bounding lines were black with white spots. It will be seen from reference to the doll of *Kó-ko-pĕ'l-i* that we have a similar circle in the same place but only four colors represented I have exhibited in the Historico-Americana Exposition an altar-cloth of the *Tcu-kü wymp-ki-a* with the same symbolism.

by an annulet made of red wool, and the back of the head is painted red with a rain-cloud ornament on either side. Around the forehead is tied a hank of yarn and upon the head there are many white feathers. The body is painted red, and across the shoulders on either side hangs a representation of a bandoleer which is double in front, and single behind. The lower legs are painted yellow and green.

Kwey-wĕ-ka-tcí-na. Pl. V Fig. 2.

The doll of *Kwey-wĕ-ka-tci-na*, the wolf-*ka-tci-na*, is a good specimen of wood carving, and is represented in a squatting posture. It is a little over seven inches in height.

The head is rounding with a projecting snout, which is slightly turned to one side and tapers forward, imparting to the face the form of the snout of the pig. The two ears are represented by black protuberances, one on each side of the top of the head. From each ear hangs a single feather (*nū-kwá-ko-ci*) painted reddish brown. The pupils of the eyes are round cavities surrounded by a broad red band. The snout is black, the lips red, and imperfect serrations represent the teeth. The remainder of the head is brown red. The neck, body and the upper arms, which are not free from the body, are of a uniform brown red color down to the waist. The forearms are black with white spots. The hands are red with indentations to mark the fingers. The left hand carries a bow and arrows and is extended forward; the right forearm is slightly raised. Around the body over the right shoulder hangs a bandoleer to which is appended a buckskin sachel. Both are stained red with iron oxide (*cú-ta*). The waist is girt with a green belt.

The lower part of the body, below and behind, is painted black without white spots. The upper legs, flanks and knees, are brown red. The lower legs, like the lower arms, are black with white spots. A hank of dark blue yarn is tied just under the knees. The upper part of the feet is green, the lower and sides bright red.

La-kón-ma-na.

The figurine of *La-kón-ma-na* is placed on the altar in the *Lá-la-kon-ti.* It has been figured and described in a paper on this ceremony [1], but I have not succeeded in getting a doll of the same. The same person is represented in the sand picture made on the floor of the room (*kib-va*) in which the *Lá-la-kon-ti* is celebrated as described and figured in the article already mentioned.

Lén-ya-ka-tcí-na.

There is in the Washington collection a beautiful doll of the Flute-*ká-tci-na*, and I have seen similar dolls in the villages, but have not purchased one of them for my collection.

There are upon the head of the specimens of these dolls, which I have seen, a number of objects similar to those placed in the pile of sand and meal before the images near the altar of the Flute-fraternity [2]. In the Washington specimen, conventionalized squash symbols also project from the top of the head. The triangular markings on the cheeks of

---

[1]) *American Anthropologist*, April 1892.

[2]) See description of the Flute-Ceremony (*A Journal of American Ethnology and Archaeology.* Vol. II. N°. 1.)

Lén-ya-ka-tcí-na remind me of *Sa-li-ko-ma-na*, but the bars on the chin are somewhat different from the curved rainbow lines of the chin of the latter.

Ma-lo-ka-tcí-na. Pl. VIII Fig. 21.

There are several specimens of the doll of this *ka-tcí-na* in the collection at Washington and in that which I have made. The doll is readily recognized and the symbolic characters are well marked. The head of the specimen before me has upon its right side a conventionalized squash ornament, made of yarn, stretched between radiating sticks and surrounded by long brilliantly colored red horse hair. On the left side of the head are tied feathers and a bunch of red horse hair. The face of this specimen is divided into a right and left side, which are differently colored and separated by a diagonal line, extending obliquely from the snout towards the right side of the face. This line is black and in it are white bands arranged in two rows. The right side of the face is green, the left yellow. Both sides are bordered by a black band, around which is a red margin on the right side and a green band on the left side of the face. The forehead is crossed by a black band in which are semicircular white spots dotted with black. A similar marking extends across the lower margin of the face in which are depicted four rectangular white marks.

The body is red, the right breast yellow and the left breast green. From these patches of colors depend marks of yellow and green. The fore left arm is green, the fore right arm yellow. The doll is represented with a white and green kilt, bordered with black. The fore legs are yellow and green, alternating with the marks on the breast. On the back of the head is painted a cloud-symbol. A distinguishing mark of this *ka-tcí-na* is the oblique black line, across the face and the two colored cheeks. I have already published an account of the dance in which this *ka-tcí-na* takes part.

Ma-zráu-ti-Io.

A figurine of *Ma-zráu-ti-Io* and of *Ma-zráu-wüq-ti* [1]) stand on the cross bar of the altar of the *Mam-zráu-ti*. They are figured and described in an account of this ceremony. [2])

Mü-yiñ-wûh.

The figurine of the Germ God is figured and described in an account of the *Lá-la-kon-ti*, a woman's ceremonial which occurs in the month of September. [3]) I have not seen a *ti-hu* of this personage and as nearly as I can learn it is not made in the pueblos.

It is of course possible to have the *ti-hus* of different *ka-tcí-nas* manufactured to order and certain men have a reputation as being clever workmen in this line. The images which the women make are ordinarily of clay and I have not seen them attempt wood carving, although they may at times do so. I attempted to have a doll or figurine of *Mü-yiñ-nûh* cut out of wood, but did not succeed being met with the reply that men know little of this deity and the women, who took part in the ceremony in which the figure was used, were as a rule reluctant to duplicate the image in clay. I am however quite sure that the figure in the *Lá-la-kon-ti* was made of wood.

---

[1]) *Ti-Io*, Youth; *wúq-ti*, married woman.
[2]) *American Anthropologist*, July, 1892.
[3]) *American Anthropologist*, April, 1892.

Má-sau-wûh.

A small doll, sometimes called *Má-sau-wûh* and sometimes by the Zuñi-name given below, has a black face with two white eyes and various colored round spots on the face similar to *Schú-ler-wit-zer* in the Zuñi dance.[1]) The back of the carved blanket of the body is covered with black cross lines which extend forward on each side. A very much soiled blanket was tied about the neck. This doll was very much delapidated and was not purchased, and only a single specimen was seen. I have seen *Má-sau-wûh* personified by the *Ta-tcúk-ti* in a public dance at Te-wa.

A helmet ascribed to *Má-sau-wûh* was painted black and upon the apex was a tuft of feathers. An annulet made of corn husks was tied around each eye and around the mouth. To the back of the mask was tied a stick to the tip of which were attached a feather and piñon boughs. The helmet of the chipmunk-*ka-tci-na* was black and a diagonal band extended across the face from left to right, colored with the four colors red, green, white, and yellow. The mask of *Kwu-wi-ko-li* was black with brown hair. The eyes were large and protuberant and there were two vertical lines of white color on each cheek. The mouth was duck-bill-shaped, painted green with red lips. Its base was girt with yellow fur. Symbols of the frog on a blue green ground were painted on the back.

Na-taé-ka. Pl. IX Fig. 30.

I have a good *ti-hu* of *Na-taé-ka* which has the same symbolic features as the masks of the same. The doll is a large one and is slightly stooping in posture. It is exceptional in that the arms and head are separate from the body and admit of motion.

The head is black prolonged into an alligator-like snout in which the mouth is cut as a deep cleft. The lips are red and the teeth brown. There is a horn on each side of the head, which is painted green below, and black at the tips, and is girt with two black bands. The eyes are raised wooden balls, black with a white iris. In the middle of the forehead there is a green arrow, pointing forward and there is a crest of feathers on the back of the head. A second specimen is figured in my plates (Pl. IX Fig. 30.)

The body is clothed with a shirt of American calico, over which is thrown a buckskin blanket and a buckskin kilt. Under this the lower part of the body and upper legs, near the thighs, are painted white with red vertical stripes. The right lower leg is yellow; the left green; both with a black garter. The feet are red.

I have examined the masks of *Na-taé-ka* used in the personification of this character,

---

[1]) There is evidence that the Zuñi *Schú-ler-wit-zer* and *Má-sau-wûh* are indentical personages. Both names were given me for the doll. The boy personifying the fire god? (*Schú-ler-wit-zer* is described in Vol. I, *Journal of American Ethnology and Archaeology*). There is a wooden figurine, in the Washington collection, which is black, dotted with variegated spots which may be a representation of the Zuñi fire-god. The feet are not painted and seem to be later additions, and the wood of which it is made is not the same as that which is always used in the manufacture of *ti-hus* by the Tusayan people.

The presence of the *Má-sau-wûh*, the fire-god, was made known to the ancient people, according to the Snake-legend, by his foot-prints on the ground.*)

*) When the ancient Mexicans in the "second festival" of the sun-god sprinkled meal before his sanctuary, the priest (chief) awaited until he saw the foot prints of the divine being in it, and then announced that the god had come. In Yucatan, as recorded by TYLOR, there is a custom of leaving a child alone at night in a place strewn with ashes. If a foot-print of an animal were found on the following morning, this animal became the guardian deity of the child. There are a number of instances which might be mentioned in various folktales of the foot-prints of deities. *Má-sau-wûh* has much in common symbolically speaking with the "Death God" of Maya-Codices.

as they were kept in a back chamber, owned by the Indian of whom I rented my room.

There are two black, two white, and one yellow *Na-taé-ka* masks which I have studied, and they all resemble each other except in color and minor details of construction.

Na-a-ma-taé-ka.[1])

The two *Na-a-ma-taé-ka* masks are made of leather painted black with projections on the side of the head made of split horns. The mouth opening betrays a double row of teeth made of twisted corn husks bent together. Within the mouth a huge red tongue of leather is placed. The lips are painted red and around them there is a white border, to which on each edge are glued stiff black hairs and downy feathers or native cotton wool.

The eyes are spherical balls tied to the head and made of buckskin. Their pupil is white, the remainder black. At their base is tied a number of feathers. The two *á-la* or horns on the head are painted green and black and at their base of attachment there is a small fragment of sheepskin wool, stained brown. A minute feather is tied to their tips. Upon the fore-head there is an arrow-head ornament painted green, with point directed forward. To the back of the head is tied a bundle of corn-husks, and a bunch of eagle-tail feathers which forms a crest-like projection. The mask helmet fits closely over the head extending down on the neck.

Pa-la-na-tac-ka.

The yellow *Na-taé-ka* is the same as the black, except that it is painted brownish yellow. The snout is slender. The eyes are black with white pupils.

Ku-etc-na-tac-ka.

The two white *Na-taé-ka* helmets are in certain important respects different from the preceeding. The upper jaw is made of a half gourd and is capable of movement on its leather support. It is manipulated with a string.

The helmet of *Ha-hai-wuq-ti*, the mother? of the monsters, which is also kept in the same room as those of *Na-taé-ka*, is of rounded shape, colored black with a white face. Around the eyes are two crescents in black, and a round red dot on each cheek.[2])

The helmet of *Wo-yá-kwa-ti* which is associated with both, *Ha-hai-wuq-ti* and *Na-taé-ka*, is interesting. It is made of leather so that it fits over the head and has more of a conical

---

[1]) SAHAGUN in the rare *Mss.* in the Madrid collection (Real Academia) gives figures of eight personifications of deities which have interested me greatly in comparison with the *Na-taé-ka* helmets and *ti-hus* which I have studied at Wal-pi. To these he gives the names *tlepalcoyutl*, *tlecoyutl*, *tlilticoyutl*, *çitlalcoyutl*, *chaniolcoyutl*, *xiuhcoyutl*, *iztaccoyutl*, and one other more elaborately figured, the name of which is doubtful to me. The colors of these in order mentioned as represented are pink, black with bright red flames, brown, brown with spots, very dark brown, blue, white, brown. I am inclined to believe that there is an intimate connection between the cardinal points and these colors and to refer the *coyutl* and *Na-taé-ka* to the same deity. In this connection the crest of feathers on the head, the form of the snout, the mouth and the teeth are interesting. The Mexican personifications are represented by covering the body, arms and legs with a skin, as well as the head. *Na-taé-ka* wears a mask. The marks on the body and appendages in Mexican representation are painted directly on the body of *Na-taé-ka* or are simply cotton wool or feathers glued to the naked skin.

I had an opportunity to trace the Mexican figures in SAHAGUN during the Historico-Americana Exposicion in 1892—93 for which I am indebted to the Delegate in charge of the document.

[2]) The readers attention is called to similar spots on the cheeks of the Mexican "God of Death?" The Maya "Death-God" sometimes has spots on the body like *Má-sau-wüh*.

than a rounded shape. The face is painted green, and the eyes are diamond-shaped black figures with white centres and black diagonal horizontal slits. The lower part of the helmet has a raised black band sewed to it and in the front part there is a rectangular red figure surrounded by a black line which forms the lips. Zigzag incisions denote the teeth. A long horsehair beard hangs down from the chin.

Arching over the apex of the helmet there is a crescent of twisted, dried corn leaves extending from ear to ear. In this at intervals, in a radiating manner, are placed feathers from the tail of the eagle. A pair of pine needles hangs over the forehead and from each projection, which forms the ears, a feather and pinon needles depend.

Wo-ya-kwa-ti-ka-tci-na is said to accompany the *Na-tać-ka(s)* and their mother, *Ha-hai-wuq-ti*, about the pueblo, at the time when they appear.

Ne-vak-ka-tcí-ní. Pl. V Fig. 4.

My *tí-hu* of this *ka-tci-na*, the Snow-*ka-tci-na*, is a very interesting piece of wood carving. The doll represents a person wearing a garment which is unlike a dance kilt or a blanket, and the whole figure is ten inches high.

The face is ornamented with two rectangles with corners replaced by *nak'-tci*-ornaments. The right side is green; the left white. The area surrounding the white rectangle is green; that surrounding the green is white. A black band extends down the middle line of the face around the lower margin and over the forehead. A projecting red and green ridge overhangs the face. In this are placed three white downy feathers. The ears are projecting appendages colored red, with feathers in them. The back of the head is white, and to it is tied a bundle of feathers, which project above the flat crown of the head. A cedar bough is tied about the neck.

The lower rim of the garment is girt by a black band, crossed by five pairs of parallel yellow lines. Alternating with these on the upper margin of the lower black band there are five pairs of triangular symbols similar to those found on marriage blankets.

The left upper arm is yellow, the right green; the left fore arm is green, the upper yellow. The hands are black. The thighs are white and the left leg is yellow; the right green, with black garters. The feet are red.

O-hó-le-ka-tcí-na. Pl. VIII Fig. 22.

A *tí-hu* of *O-hó-le-ka-tci-na* which was seen and sketched, but not purchased, has a square face rounded in front and crossed by a transverse band from ear to ear. The face itself is colored green with a black lower border. The medial line of this transverse band is blue with two vertical white bands near the medial line, and two of the same color at each end. The eyes have a black centre with white iris.

Crossing this variously colored transverse band in the middle vertical position, an upright bar of blue with a red margin, surrounded by a black line is painted. Upon the top of the head there is tied a bunch of feathers. The ears are represented by projections and through each of them is stuck a single feather.

The body is red without markings, the right upper arm yellow, and the left upper arm green. The right fore-arm is green, the left fore-arm yellow.

A blanket, carved in wood, is white above and green below, bordered with black block ornamentation. The upper legs are red, the right lower leg yellow, the left green, both surrounded with black garters. The soles of the feet and the sides of the same are red.

Pañ-wa-ka-tcí-na. Pl. X Fig. 33 (Pl. VII Fig. 14?)

Pañ-wā, the mountain sheep-[1]) *ka-tcí-na*, is represented by a well carved *tí-hu*, illustrating many of the symbolic characters of this interesting personage.

The top of the head has two curved, slightly twisted white horns, along the front of which are zigzag green lines. Upon these are fastened little clusters of downy breath feathers. The top of the head is painted white with a semicircular projecting rim over the face. The under surface of this rim is painted with parallel lines extending its whole length and colored red, black, yellow, black, green, and red, beginning with the face and extending to the outer rim. Three black *na-kwá-ko-ci* are tied to the rim of this projection. The back of the head is painted red.

The face is green with a black lower border in which are four white spots. In the middle line of the face there are two black triangles with angles placed together, forming an hour glass figure. The eyes are represented by black slits. There is a single black spot on each cheek. The snout is duck-bill-shaped, black above, white below with black spots and girt by a black band. The appendages to the sides of the head are two white frustra of cones painted white, slightly concave on the outside and crossed by green bands. These resemble conventionalized squash blossoms.

The neck is white, body red with a yellow left, and green right breast. From the left breast there hangs down a yellow and green *ka-tcí-na* mark; from the right a green and yellow. Similar colors occur also on the back over the shoulder blades. The left arm is green, the fore arm yellow with black borders. The upper right arm is yellow, the fore arm green with black border and both hands black.

The *ka-tcí-na* wears a dance-kilt, cut in wood, with a white upper and green lower portion. Its fore arm is surrounded by a black margin with black rectangles. The junction of the kilt on the right hand side is elaborately decorated with four rectangles in which, on a white field, are several red lines.

The left leg is green with yellow and red garter, the right leg is yellow with red and green garter. There is a black hank of wool tied on each leg. The right foot is green on the upper side. Both feet are red. A few strands of red yarn, tied on the right side, surrounds the waist above the blanket.

Pa-tüc-uñ-a-la. Pl. IX Fig. 25.

A doll of this personage, who is said to come in the *So-yál-a-na* (December-ceremony), has three curved horns on the head and the body painted pink, with four white bars on the breast.

Pa-lá-pik-in.

Pa-lá-pik-in is a *Wá-wac-ka-tcí-na* [2]) and can be recognized by the rectangular frame-

---

[1]) Erroneously called *goat* in *Journal of American Ethnology and Archaeology* Vol. II.

[2]) For description of other *Wá-wac* or racing *Ka-tci-nas* and account of the event see *Bull. Essex Institute* 1892.

work, one on each side of the head. There is a doll of this in the Bureau of Ethnology Collection in Washington.

La-pük-ti. Pl. XI Fig. 40.

La-pük-ti is recognized by a black face with two oblique white bars on each cheek and three parallel white bars on the forehead. In the *tí-hu* which I have in my collection cedar bark is fastened over the head.

Paú-ti-va-ka-tcí-na. Pl. VIII Fig. 23.

The doll of *Paú-ti-va* is a little over eight inches tall and is represented with a blanket extending from the shoulders to the knees. The head is cylindrical, and to the flat top which is painted black is tied a cluster of yellow and white feathers. The forehead slightly projects over the face and is painted black. The back of the head is of the same color. The lower edge of the face is girt by a black band in which are four white elongated spots. The face is green, with a dumb-bell-shaped, black figure lined with yellow, extending across the median line of the upper part.

The two ears are large, rounded processes, extending from the forehead band to that on the lower side of the face. Its rim is painted red, and the figures on the two faces are identical in shape and colors. Near the head they are white with a white square occupying the middle of the ear. The rounded rim is black and the colors of both ears are identical. *Paú-ti-va* has a bird-like snout painted green above and below, with the lips red. The line of the mouth is obscurely indicated.

A slight furrow indicates the position of the neck which is painted red. The breadth of the shoulders is about the same as that of the head. The body is represented as clothed in a woman's blanket over a ceremonial dance kilt. The upper border of the woman's blanket is adorned with a broad black band near the neck. This border is serrated along the lower rim. On each side it is crossed by two vertical green lines, and on either side of the medial line of the back, there are two diagonals with a yellow border within which is a black band, lining a red diagonal field upon which is a white cross. The lower rim of the blanket is ornamented with a similar black band and four vertical green lines, with two diagonal and three pairs of black triangles on the upper rim. The space between these two black lines or that in which the triangles lie, is white. The body on the front which is shown by the blanket being thrown back is painted bright red from neck to waist, but the arms are not separated from the body. The right forearm is yellow with a black border and fringes; the left green with the same colored border.

The representation of the ceremonial blanket is carved from the wood and is green with an elaborate border above and below. The lower border is a narrow black band with four rectangles in black. The upper border is composed of black, yellow, and red parallel lines in the midst of which are four black, diamond-shaped figures. The vertical border on the right side is ornamented with red and white *nak'-tci* (rain-clouds) and black lines.

The left leg is green, the rigt yellow. The two feet are red, but the upper part of the right foot is green.

Pü'-ü-koñ. Pl. V Fig. 5.

The *tí-hu* of *Pü'-ü-koñ*, the „war god" is eight inches tall. It is destitute of limbs, with a uniform diameter from the shoulders to the hips. The head is surmounted by a conical projection, two inches and a half high, painted green, at the top of which is a feather. The head itself is painted black, with white rings for eyes and mouth. Upon either cheek there are two short parallel vertical white marks, a constant decoration both on fetishes and *tí-hus* of *Pü'ü-koñ*. The ears are represented by two red colored lappets. On the back of the head there are four parallel white lines, and upon the top of the head, radiating from the base of the conical green continuation, there are three pairs of white lines, two of which arise from just above the forehead, and the remaining pairs at equal distances radially on the top of the head.

The body is painted black and covered with white lines which cross each other diagonally. The arms are closely pressed to the sides of the body, and girt with yellow bands on the upper outer sides, while the hands are green. The base is painted white, and is flat as if cut off at the hips.

There is in the Washington collection an interesting doll of the war-god which has the form of a bicephalic person. This doll evidently represents the twin war-gods, and is instructive to study in connection with the relationship of these gods. It is painted black over the whole body with the exception of the characteristic white marks which, as we have described, are found on the face and body of this personage. The distribution of these marks in the two-headed specimen in the Washington collection, is as follows: There are two parallel vertical white marks on each cheek of each face and two similar bars on the arms and legs. Two white bars occur on each of the two shoulder blades, and two on each breast on each side. There are also two bars on the lower part of the body on each side. The head is crowned by a conical appendage painted green, upon the apex of which is a feather. This conception of the twins is interesting from an anatomical side, and there could be no more definite way of indicating their relationship.

I have not yet succeeded in getting a doll of the twin-brother of *Pü'-ü-kong*, nor of the maternal ancestor *Kó-ky-an-wuq-ti*, the Spider-woman. Of the latter however I have two fetishes, made of clay. The body of both is spherical, but otherwise there is no marked symbolism.

Si-o-hu-mís-ka-tcí-na.

An instructive doll of the collection is called the Zuñi *Hu-mís-ka-tcí-na*[1]. Like the *Hú-mis* already described, this also bears a *nák-tci* on its head, but the form of this *nák-tci* is very different from that of the doll last described. The *nák-tci* is made of a piece of thin wood and is of rectangular shape with three rounded elevations, separated by intervals on the upper edge. The same semicircular field surrounded by a rainbow occupies the middle of the *nák-tci*, just above the helmet. This semicircular field is colored yellow, and the rainbow-lines, surrounding it, are black, red, black, and green. Three white marks occur in the black band between the red and the green.

The three rounded elevations on the upper margin of the *nák-tci* are painted green with a black border. Just at their bases the tablet is crossed by parallel lines, black, green, black, red, black, and yellow, counting from the upper to the lower line in the series. The surface of the *nák-tci* is painted black, and on either side there is a white figure of growing corn.

[1]) For a colored plate of *Si-ó-hu-mis*, see *A Journal of American Ethnology and Archaeology*. Vol. II, N°. 1.

Just opposite the line of contact of the visor of the helmet with the *nák-tci* on either side the green, black, yellow, black, and red lines of the rainbow semicircle are continued to the rim of the *nák-tci.* There is a yellow flower-symbol depicted on the lateral wings of the *nák-tci*, adjoining the face and the lower rim of the wings is bordered with red.

The back of the *nák-tci* is painted in the same colors as the front and the three rounded elevations are each tipped with a single feather.

The visor of the helmet is painted with parallel crescent lines: red, black, yellow, black, and red. The black band near the outer rim has the well known white spots which occur in most rainbow symbols.

The face of the helmet is divided by a median broad black line into two regions, the right green, the left red. This median band is crossed by ten parallel white lines. The red side of the face is bordered by a black line surrounded by a green, and the green side is girt by a black band surrounded by a red line. The eyes are represented by black transverse marks and there are four triangular tooth-like markings in black on each side of the face, near its union with the wings of the *nák-tci.*

The back of the head has a pinkish color and in the middle of it is represented a single green *O'-mow-ûh* (raincloud) outlined with black, out of which lines (rain-symbols) are represented. Three zigzag lightning snakes are depicted above this cloud. The neck is girt by a bough of piñon, and to the back of the head over the *O'-mow-ûh*-symbol a bunch of feathers is tied.

The arms are tightly pressed to the body and not separate from it. The body is painted black, the arm having a green band. The *tí-hu* wears a cotton kilt formerly painted white and green, with a black border, and a red sash. The hips are painted red, the legs above the knees black. Each leg is green in color and has a red line girting its knee. From the red garter hang numerous parallel red lines, while the soles and sides of the feet are likewise red in color. The heel bands used in dances are represented by white painted marks in which are depicted black crosses on the back of the foot.

Su-mai-ko-lis.

I have already described a ceremony in Ha-no which pertains to the *Su-mai-ko-lis.* The exact signification of this celebration I have not yet been able to decipher, but I have gathered some information in relation to these personages. They are said to be gnomes or wizards and are reputed to be blind. It is also said that they have wooden hands and can change themselves into trees. They wear a girdle which is composed of cedar and corn leaves and are said to have a conical hat with plumes. In a dance in which they appear a great fire was formerly kindled and one of these personages jumped into the fire, but was not burned. There is need of more research in regard to these personages. The legends connected with them recall certain ceremonies which take place among primitive people in midsummer. Among the San Domingo Indians we have also similar woodgods, whose hands are also said to be made of wood. More research is necessary however, to determine whether they are related. I have the song of the *Su-mai-ko-lis* preserved on a cylinder of the phonograph.

The celebration of the *Su-mai-ko-lis* has only been seen in Ha-no, although it probably exists in other Tusayan pueblos. Coming as it does not far from the time of the summer solstice and the fact of their association with fire, make them suggestive objects of study.

Whether their summer-rite [1]) is a modified ceremony of the summer-fire, remains for later research to determine. I have no doll of the *Su-mai-ko-lis*, nor have I been able to obtain information that such exists, but I have reason to suppose that the images of the *Su-mai-ko-lis* are sometimes fashioned.

Sá-li-ko-ma-na. Pl. VI Fig. 10, Pl. IX Fig. 28 & Pl. X Fig. 31.

Dolls of *Sá-li-ko-ma-na* are among the most numerous which the children have. They are found of all degree of complication from simple decorated flat slabs to elaborately clothed dolls with complicated *nák-tci*. A constant feature among them all is some kind of terraced head dress and a rainbow crescent about the mouth.

The best *Sá-li-ko-ma-na* which I have [2]) is a squatty figure, the head of which has a U-shaped face painted white, bearing an elaborate double *nák-tci*. The forehead is crossed by a raised band, at the ends of which there are clusters of feathers and dark red fur. The raised band is black with white rectangular spots and represents the ear of corn. From its middle, just above the nose, hangs a fragment of abalone [3]). This ornament (Haliotis) is a constant one in most of the best *ti-hus* of *Sá-li-ko* and is often represented by a ring on tile and pottery decorations. The shell of the Haliotis is very commonly worn by *Ka-tci-na* dancers.

The mouth is surrounded by a rainbow semi-circle of red color bordered with black lines, the mouthopening being indicated by a small semicircle from which radiate three black lines enclosing a yellow, red, blue, and green zone. The eyes are indicated by rectangular marks, a black border enclosing a yellow within which, on the left eye, there is a black band. The right eye however has some variation, a blue line taking the place of the yellow, by which from a distance it seems as if this eye were black throughout. This difference in the color of the eyes is almost constant among *ti-hus* of *Sa-lí-ko-ma-na*. The cheeks are marked by a red triangle with three inner red triangles. This symbol is often replaced by a red spot on each cheek.

The arrangement of the different cloud symbols, rainbow and other head ornaments can best be seen by a consultation of the figure. The reader's attention is called to the two squash emblems on their margin which is a constant feature on the head decorations of *Sá-lí-ko-ma-na*. This emblem here appears as a wooden stalk with the unfolding flower, made of red wool stretched from radiating sticks. It is to be noticed that they appear in almost identically the same position as the whorls of hair on the heads of unmarried women at the present day and on the heads of certain men who personify female *Ka-tci-na-* or *Ka-tci-na-ma-nas*.

The body of *Sá-li-ko-ma-na* is covered by feathers arranged longitudinally with the shaft pointing upwards. One is tempted to regard this as a survival of the feather-garments in which certain traditional personages were clothed. *Sá-li-ko-ma-na* has long black hair down her back. The legs are short and stumpy, the right yellow, the left green, and the feet are red.

---

1) For an account of their ceremony see *A Journal of American Ethnology and Archaeology*. Vol. II. N⁰. 1. The statement in the note p. 35 of their fire-ceremonial is erroneous and is due to the omission of the word "formerly" before "celebrate(d)". I owe this information to Mr. Stephen.

2) The other forms which I have are figured in the plates. The *Sá-li-ko-ta-ka* and *Sá-li-ko-ma-na* here described are figured in "*El Centenario*".

3) At times when from their extreme rarity shells were very costly, the women made clay imitations, many of which were very cleverly done. Some of these can be found now among the people of Wál-pi.

Passing now to *ti-hus* of *Sá-li-ko-ma-na* in which the details are less perfectly carried out, we find many of the same symbolic designs represented. The feature most commonly present is the rainbow mouth, the terraced *nák-tci*, the square variegated eyes, and the conventionalized squash blossom. The body is commonly crossed by longitudinal red lines and is ordinarily painted white.

Whether the white lines which one finds so commonly on the bodies of *ti-hus*, is a conventionalized feather garment or not, is a question which is very difficult to answer. Judging from the most perfect *ti-hu* of *Sá-li-ko-ma-na* which I have, it would seem that such a theory is possible, but I am not able as yet to make up my mind definitely on that point. In this connection the markings on the body of the great feathered serpent are significant, but from the priests whom I have interrogated I have obtained a very different interpretation of the last mentioned symbols.

Sá-lí-ko-ta-ka.

This most interesting personage in Ho-pi-folklore is represented in my collection of *ti-hus* by a huge doll, the largest which I have. In the celebration of the advent of the Zuñi *Shá-la-ko*, which I take to be the same as the Ho-pi *Sá-lī-ko*, he is represented as a giant, and his mask is borne aloft by a man concealed within. This idea is faithfully carried out in the construction of my *ti-hu*, in which the small body is carved inside the log of wood out of which the body of *Sá-lī-ko* is cut. The height of the *ti-hu* with the crest is only a few inches short of three feet.

The head is crowned by a fan-shaped crest of feathers united by a string, and raised from the back of the head. The top and back of the head are covered with sheep's-wool, stained black. There is on either side of the head a horn, girt by green and black bands.

The face is painted with black bands for the eyes and prominent black eyeballs at their inner edges. The lower rim of the face is crossed by parallel lines of black, yellow, black, red, and black. In the upper black line there are white spots. This decoration evidently is a conventional rainbow-symbol. There is a long projecting black snout painted green above and below and with red sides, crossed by a number of pairs of vertical green bands. The snout is tied to the face with cloth in a very skilful manner. From the head there hangs a string down the back, from which at intervals breath feathers are tied. Around the neck there is a collar composed of little bundles of black feathers tied by buckskin thongs, and standing out at right angles.

The *Sá-lī-ko-ta-ka* wears a white embroidered ceremonial blanket, similar to that given by a man to his wife as a marriage present. This is tied by the upper corners on the right shoulders, where there are also tassels and feathers as in certain ceremonial blankets. Arms are not represented under the blanket, but in the little figure, carved within, all the main parts of the body are faithfully carved, and without exception the figure cut inside the *Sá-li-ko* is one of the best examples of *ti-hu*-woodcarving with which I am familiar. It is painted white with a black zone about the loins and wears elaborate green moccasins. The lower legs are painted yellow.

Si-o-sa-li-ko.[1]) Pl. VIII Fig. 19, Pl. XI Fig. 37 & 43.

Another doll the name of which I am ignorant, has upon the head radiating slabs of

[1]) The name *Si-ó-sa-li-ko* or *sha-li-ko* is applied by some of the priests to a doll with radiating sunflower-

wood colored red and tipped with black, with white spots. The face is green and around each eye, which is very protuberant, there is a red rectangular figure bordered by a black band in which are white spots. Various names have been given me for this *ka-tci-na*, but I am doubtful as to its true name. The radiating slabs recall the sunflower emblem or may be conventionalized feathers. The name *Si-o* (Zuñi, *Shá-la-ko*) is commonly applied to this figurine.

Soi-yok-ma-na. Pl. VI Fig. 6 & Pl. IX Fig. 26.

Appears in the *Po-wum-ûh*-ceremony in March.

Ta-lá-tum-si. [1])

I have the following notes on the figurine of *Ta-lá-tum-si*, which figures in the celebration of the *Na-ác-nai-ya* or headwashing of the novice (*q. v.*)

The figurine is wooden, eighteen inches high and wears a miniature white mantle with girdle, in which are thrust two sets of *pa-ho*(s). The face is flat, of a yellow color; hair black. The diameter of the base of the figurine is ten inches. I have never seen the image of *Ta-lá-tum-si*, and my information is derived from Mr. STEPHEN. [2]) who identifies this as the Dawn-(*tá-la*) woman.

Tá-la-wiq-pi-ki. Pl. X Fig. 32.

A lightning-god with zigzag symbol of lightning from the rain cloud and rainbow carried over the head. Compare legends of animal nature of the rainbow.

Tcú-a-wymp-ki-ya.

Dolls of different priesthoods are commonly met with in some of the Tusayan pueblos. In the Washington collection a *ti-hu* of the *Tcú-a-wymp-ki-ya* is well marked. A doll of this priesthood, the snake fraternity, may readily be identified by the figure of the snake on the kilt and the characteristic arrow figures and parallel lines. [3])

---

sticks on the top of the head, two lateral horns, one on each side, an arrow on the forehead, and semicircular lines on the cheeks and the middle line of the face. These dolls commonly have the conventional feather diagonals on the body. I am doubtful as to the identification of this doll.

[1]) The ceremonies connected with the *Ta-lá-tum-si* have already been described elsewhere, *Journal of Amer. Folk Lore*, Vol. V. N°. XVIII.

[2]) See ceremony of the *Na-ác-nai-ya op. cit.* Mr. STEPHEN derives *Ta-lá-tum-si* from *tá-la*, dawn and *tum-si*, married woman without children.

[3]) The figures of the snake in the *Codex Cortesianus* have in some instances similar parallel marks on the body. I have seen on a kilt in one of the pueblos of the Middle mesa of the Hopi an identical arrangement of these marks as in the figures of the Codex. It would seem from the account of a Mexican ceremonial in honor of the plumed snake in Acosta, and from the *Codex Cortesianus* that the Mayas and Mexican priests of this animal wore in some of their ceremonials helmets, bearing the characteristic symbolism of the plumed snake. Such does not exist in the Hopi snake-ceremony of summer, unless we look upon the facial decoration and feathers as of that nature.

My attention has been called by Dr. SELER to figures and descriptions in SAHAGUN of priests with snakes in their mouths, but there is little resemblance in the symbols worn by these priests, *Maçatecatl*, and the *Tcú-a-wymp-ki-ya*. In some respects the *Maçatecatl* remind me of the "stick swallowers," of the Navajos and Zuñi. I hope to reproduce SAHUGUNS figures and descriptions in a subsequent publication. For description of the ceremony of the month *Quecholli* see GOMARRA p. 199 "*toman las culebras a manos*," "*toman eso mismos las culebras del cascabel*"; also SERNA, p. 91: Manuel de Ministros de Indios etc. *Documentos ineditos*. Tomo CIV.

Ta-táñ-ai-ya.

I have studied several dolls of *Ta-táñ-ai-ya*, two of which are in the collection at Washington. The single specimen of which I have a sketch, is a small one of cylindrical shape, the head being but slightly separated from the body by a shallow groove. Both, body and head, are surrounded by parallel bands of white, black, yellow, and green colors. There are two straight horn-like elevations on the top of the head which are also girt with parallel bands of different colors. The two specimens in Washington have similar colored bands and horns.

Tcu-kú-wymp-ki-ya. Pl. XI Fig. 42.

There is a doll in my collection representing a member of the *Tcuc-ku-tû*, one division of this priesthood, and also another representing the *Pai-a-kai-a-muh* [1]). In the former the body and face are painted yellow throughout, with the exception of a band about the waist, which is blue. Hair is represented by black sheepskin, and the face is marked by two parallel red bands one crossing the eyes, the other the mouth. Around the neck is fastened a necklace of berries. Strung on the shoulder is a small bundle of native bread and piñon needles. In its hands it carries a wooden bowl painted white with black decoration.

The doll representing the Tewan gluttons, *Pai-a-kai-a-muh*, Pl. VI Fig. 9, has the face painted green and the body white. Upon the head are two projections, painted with white and black bands alternating with fragments of corn husks. The back of the head is covered with corn smut, and to each ear is tied a small fragment of uncolored corn-husk. The body is girt with two black lines and the arms and legs with three bands of the same color. The feet are painted red.

Although the majority of these dolls are made in imitation of mythical personages, one often finds imitations of the different priesthoods cut out of wood in the same way. The clowns and gluttons above mentioned belong to this category. I have also seen in the collection at Washington a figure of a Snake-priest painted and adorned in the same way as the priests are dressed in the ceremonials. There is perhaps no better means of studying the different personages who appear in ceremony than by a consideration of these dolls. The custom reminds one somewhat of a degenerate art in Mexico of illustrating types of people by clay images, and it is possibly not unlike what we find in the so-called Tanagra-figures.

The dolls representing Tewan gluttons in the Washington collection are good examples of wood carving and much more elaborately ornamented than the single specimen which I have. Only one of these however has the corn husks still appended to the horns of the head. There are in the same collection also a number, *Tcuc-ku-tü*, which in general resemble the specimen which I have described. In all I have examined fourteen specimens of dolls of this priesthood.

Ta-tcúk-ti [2]).

In looking over the dolls which have been referred to the mud-heads, *Ta-tcük-ti*, I find

[1]) Tewan *Tcu-kú-wymp-kia*. See photograph in *Journal of Ethnology*. Vol. II.
[2]) A division of the *Tcu-kú-wymp-ki-ya*.

several specimens on exhibition and others among the duplicates. In some of these there are on each cheek two parallel marks, each of which, in one or two instances, has a crook at one end. One of the mud-heads has the body ornamented with red and white vertical lines. It is without legs, and from the fact that it has the two knoblike appendages to the head and the marks on the cheek, I have identified it as a *Ta-tcúk-ti.* Several of the dolls of these priests have the legs painted in bright colors. I have not seen any attempt at painting on the legs of the men who take the part of these priests in the dance.

Ta-cáb-kā-tci-na. Pl. VIII Fig. 20.

Very many of the dolls have the general name of *Ta-cáb* or Navajo-*Ka-tci-na.* These all agree in certain general characteristics. A common form of Navajo doll is one with two diagonal lines extending across the face forming an inverted V-shaped body with angle between the eyes and extremities on the lower portion of the head. In most of these dolls the lines upon the body are longitudinal instead of vertical. In one doll of the Navajo-*Ka-tci-na* the eyes are painted hook-shaped with rounding lateral ends. In the masks which I have observed and which are worn by men in personifying the person represented by the doll, the face is crossed by a white line extending from the nose across the cheek to the jaw.

Tcüb-ka-tcí-na.

The dolls of the Antelope-*ka-tci-na* assume several shapes, one of the best of which is decorated as follows: The face is painted green with a rectangular black mark surrounded by a red margin in the middle of the forehead. There are two black slits representing the eyes, and below them two large round red eyes with black pupils. The significance of this will be seen by a consultation of my account of *Sá-li-ko*-dolls where the latter are protuberant and lie on the inner edge of the slits. A protruding red ridge overhangs the forehead. There are wooden lightning-symbols on the top of the head, and two squash symbols one on each side of the same part of the body. The cluster of feathers on the top and back of the head are brown and not highly colored. The mouth is duck-bill shaped and the lower rim of the face has four white marks in a black band. The body and legs are red, and the waist is covered with a white cotton dance kilt. The right lower leg is brown, the left yellow. Both the feet are painted red.

Dú-mai-ka-tcí-na.

A little doll, which was made by one of the Ho-pi, was different in several particulars from many others which I have seen. The ornamentation of its face is as follows. The long middle line of the face is a black bar rising at right angles from a cross band which separates the chin from the upper part of the face. The left side of the face is yellow; the right green. The chin is red with a black rectangle in the middle. Across the forehead extends a black band.

Tü-tum-che-ka-tcí-na.

The doll of this *Ka-tci-na* has a green face with two square eyes lined with black with white interiors. It has two slabs on the top of the head, one of which is a symbolic lightning-slab, the other the notched stick used in the accompaniment of the song of the dance by the *Ka-tci-na-ma-nas.* Hair is represented by cotton wool and the bunch of feathers on the head are highly colored red, green, and yellow.

The body is painted red with a green patch on the right and a yellow on the left breast. From these extend green and yellow markings to the waist.

The dance kilt is carved in wood represented as standing stiffly outward, painted green with black border. The girdle is white with diagonal line. The legs are red and the feet green on the upper side.

A doll of this *Ka-tcí-na* has the face crossed by a diagonal stair-like mark extending from the upper left hand corner to the lower right hand side. The face is green and crossed by parallel bars of red, yellow, and black. Along the middle line of the face there is a black band. The two ears are painted red. Dolls with terraced lines painted on the face are very common among the Indians, and various names have been given me for them. I am not yet prepared to say however, whether they all belong to the same *Ka-tcí-na* or not, but there is every likelihood that they do.

Yó-a-ta.

A carved image of *Yó-a-ta* is figured and described in the account of the *Lá-la-kon-ti* (*q.v.*). At the time that article was written, I was ignorant of the name of the wooden figurine which stood by the side of *La-kón-ma-na* or between her and the last on the extreme left (*Ka-lék-to-ka*). The name *Yó-a-ta* has now been given me for this personage.

Wu-pá-mo-ka-tcí-na [1]). Pl. VI Fig. 8.

I have a very good *ti-hu* of *wu-pá-mo* which gives an excellent idea of this *Ka-tcí-na.*

The face is rotund and the head lenticular. The shoulders are represented with very broad arms which are exceptionally free from the body. The proportions of the legs and the adornment of the dance kilt is better than in most *ti-hus.*

The face is divided into three regions, a lower part forming almost a semicircle of the face and a quadrant on either side. The lower half of the face is painted black and a broad median line separates the two quadrants on the upper hemisphere. Two daubs of white paint are found on the upper rim of the black lower hemisphere, and there are two white marks in the black median division. The left quadrant of the face is yellow, the right green. The eyes are spherical, protuberant balls with a black pupil surrounded by a white zone outside. The long pointed snout is black above, with red lips below, and white zigzag-painted mouth-opening. The tongue is represented by a piece of red buckskin hanging at the tip of the snout. The back of the head is white. Around the rim of the face there project radially five stiff appendages, three of which are spatulate wooden slabs (omitted in the figure) and three round sticks covered with feathers. Of the former slabs one arises from the top of the head and the other two from the points at a level with the eyes. The three sticks with feather attachments alternate with these, and a cluster of feathers is tied to the back of the head. Around the neck there is tied a skin-collar with the hair outside.

The body above the kilt is bright red, tapering uniformly to the waist. On the right breast there is a green patch, from which extend yellow and green parallel marks, and

---

[1]) Possibly derived from *wú-po*, great; *O'-mow-ûh*, cloud.

on the left a yellow patch of color with the same marks. Similar colored paint is also found on the two shoulder blades. The upper arms are both red. The right with a yellow, the left with a green line on the outside. The right forearm is yellow, the left green. The line of the back bone is indicated by a groove.

The figure has a dance-kilt carved in wood which is white near the waist and green below, bordered by a black band with square black rectangles. The embroidered region is indicated by parallel lines of black and yellow. The right leg is green painted with red, green and yellow garters. The left leg is yellow with red, yellow and green garters.

In the preceeding pages I have in one or two instances introduced statements derived from hearsay. In such cases I have carefully stated that fact. While I have no cause to distrust explanations which are given by the honest priests I think we ought to regard them with great care. Traditional explanations given by priests are of great importance but they may or may not be true explanations. It is asking too much to expect one race or tribe to account for the existence of beliefs as widely spread as the human race. The problem is more complex than this would indicate. Local theories may have arisen to account for certain ceremonials, or for certain systems of mythology. Germs of truth may have come down from the most remote antiquity, but it is certainly unscientific to stop at these explanations for almost universal beliefs. I am in doubt whether any one can explain the reason why Mokis, Zuñis or any of our American aborigines hold certain beliefs or practice certain ceremonials, but a good way to approximate an explanation is by a comparison of similar practices among all the ceremonies of the ancient culture. Such comparative studies mean the collection of a vast number of facts.

MADRID, February 1893.

EXPLANATION OF THE PLATES.

PLATE V.

Fig. 1. Hu-mís-ka-tcí-na.
„ 2. Kwéy-we „
Fig. 3. Há-ka-to-ka-tcí-na.
„ 4. Nevák „
„ 5. Pü'-ü-koñ.

PLATE VI.

Fig. 6. Soi-yók-ma-na.
„ 7. Hă-wuq-ti.
„ 8. Wu-pà-mo.
Fig. 9. Tcu-kú-wymp-ki-ya (Pai-a-ký-a-muh).
„ 10. Sá-li-ko-ma-na.
„ 11. O'-mow-ûh.

PLATE VII.

Fig. 12. Kwa-hús-a-lék-to-ka.
„ 13. Tcüb-ka-tcí-na (page 71).
„ 14. Pañ'-wa-ka-tcí-na.
Fig. 15. Ko-ho-ní-no-ka-tcí-na.
„ 16. He-hé-a „
„ 17. Hó-chan-e „

PLATE VIII.

Fig. 18. He-hé-a-ka-tcí-na.
„ 19. Si-o-sá-li-ko „
„ 20. Ta-cab- „
Fig. 21. Ma-lo- ka-tcí-na.
„ 22. O'-ho-le „
„ 23. Pau-ti-wa „

PLATE IX.

Fig. 24. Aí-wo-to-to.
„ 25. Pa-tüc-ùñ-a-la.
„ 26. Soi-yók-ma-na.
„ 27. Ha-hai-wüq-ti.
Fig. 28. Sá-li-ko ma-na.
„ 29. A-váte-ka-tcí-na.
„ 30. Na-tác-ka.

PLATE X.

Fig. 31. Sa-li-ko-ma-na and He-hé-a with phallic symbols on the breast and abdomen.
„ 32. Ta-la-wiq-pi-ki.
„ 33. Pañ-wa-ka-tci-na.
Fig. 34. Tca-kwaí-na.
„ 35. Hónê-tca-ka-tci-na.
„ 36. See note 1 pg. 57.

PLATE XI.

Fig. 37. Si-o-S(h)á-li-ko.
„ 38. Sí-o-ka-tci-na.
„ 39. Có-tük-i-nuñ-wû.
„ 40. La-pük'-ti.
Fig. 41. Du-màs-ka-tci-na.
„ 42. Tcúc-kü-ti (Tcu-kü-wymp-ki-ya).
„ 43. Sí-o-sa-li-ko.

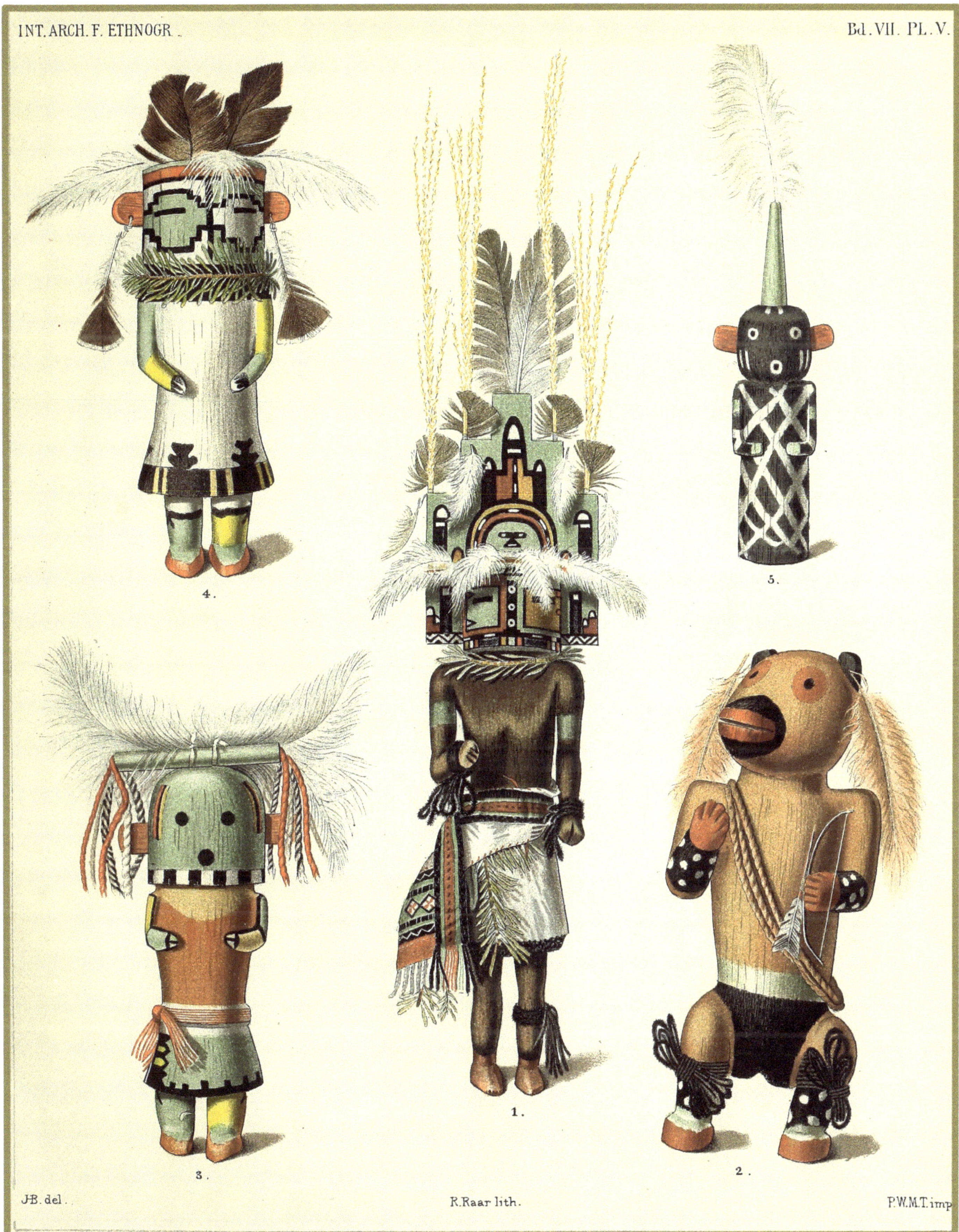
INT. ARCH. F. ETHNOGR.
Bd. VII. PL. V.
4.
5.
1.
3.
2.
J-B. del.
R. Raar lith.
P.W.M.T. imp.

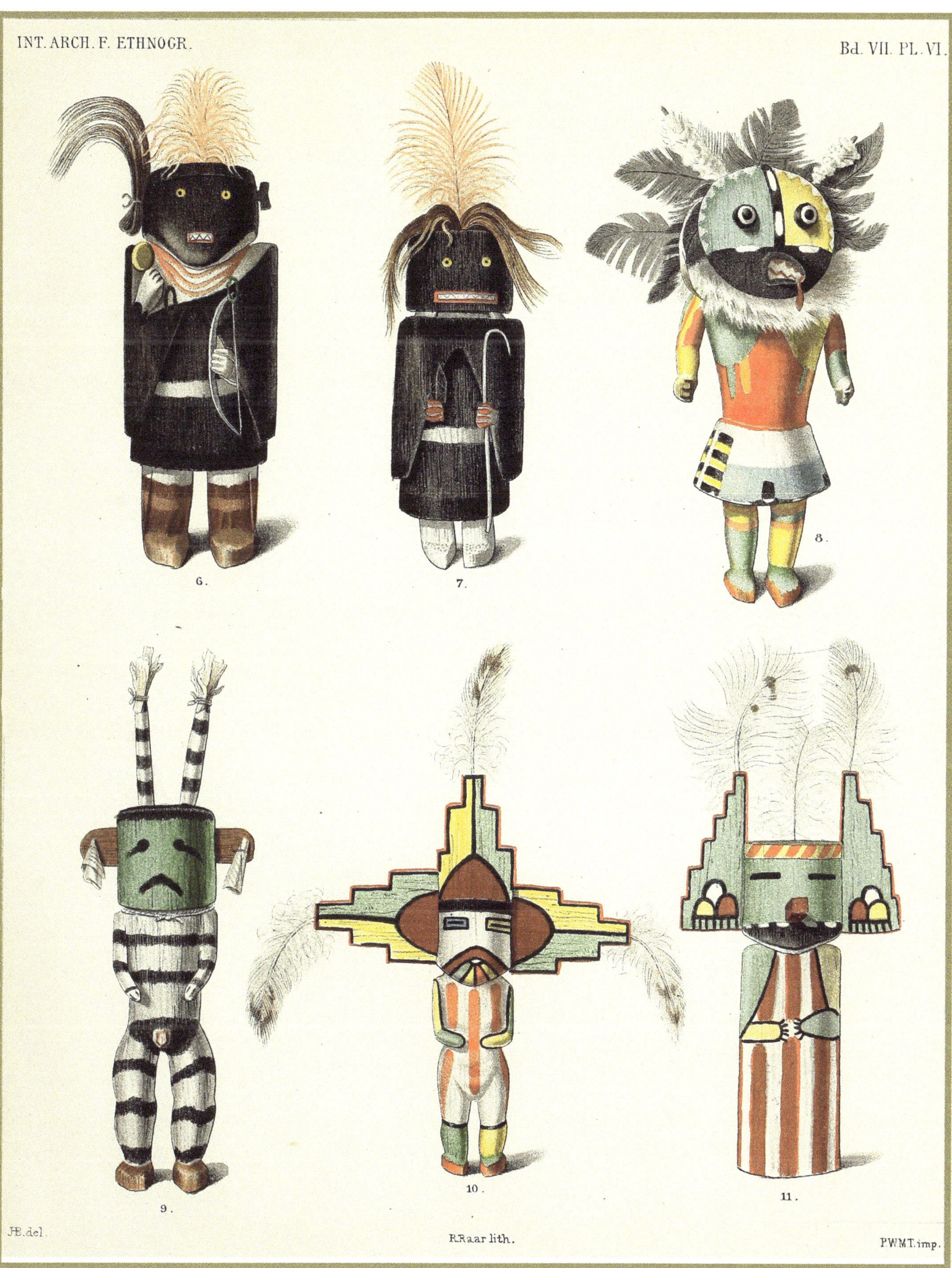

J.B. del. R. Raar lith. P.W.M.T. imp.

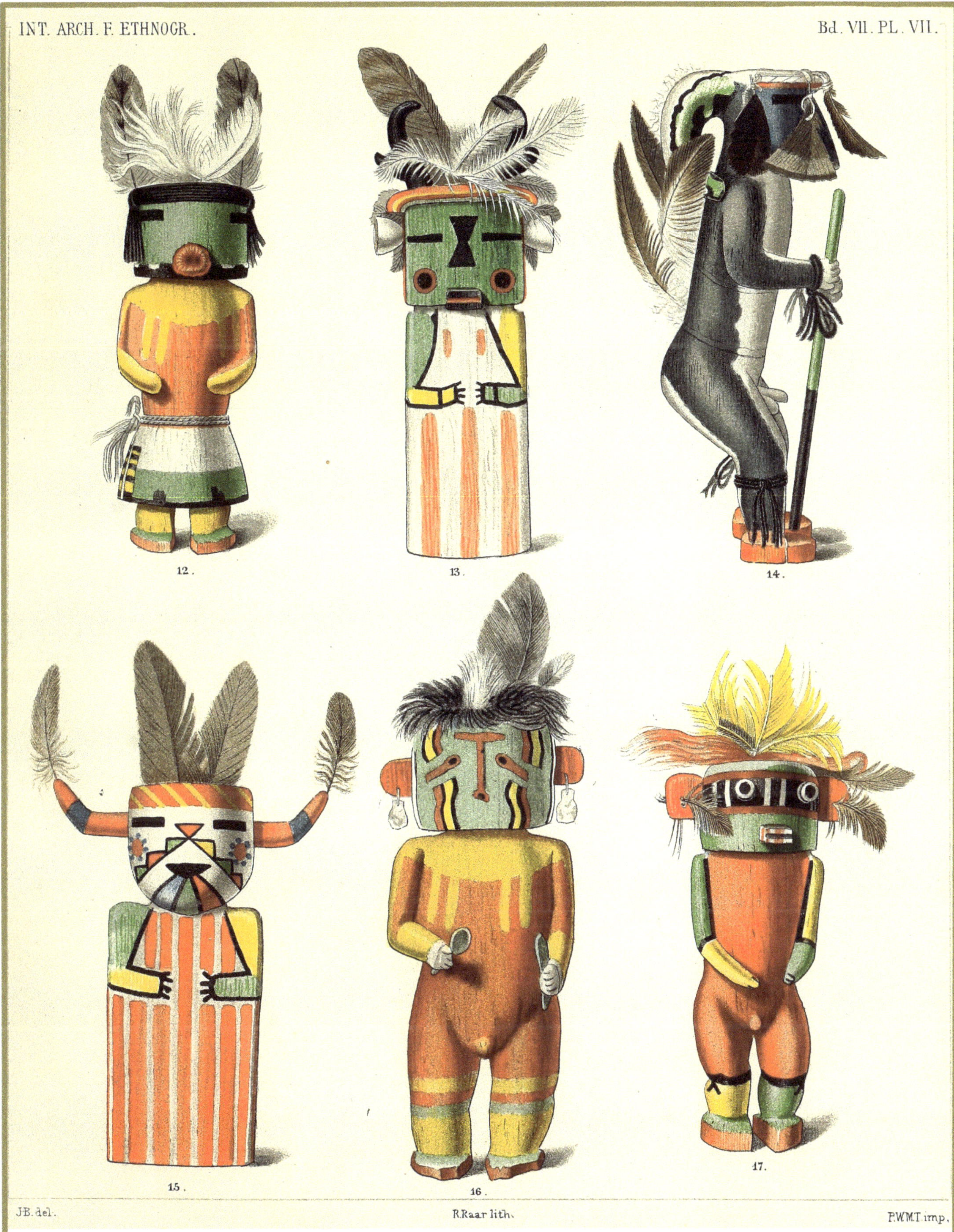
INT. ARCH. F. ETHNOGR.
Bd. VII. PL. VII.
12.
13.
14.
15.
16.
17.
J.B. del.
R. Raar lith.
P.W.M.T. imp.

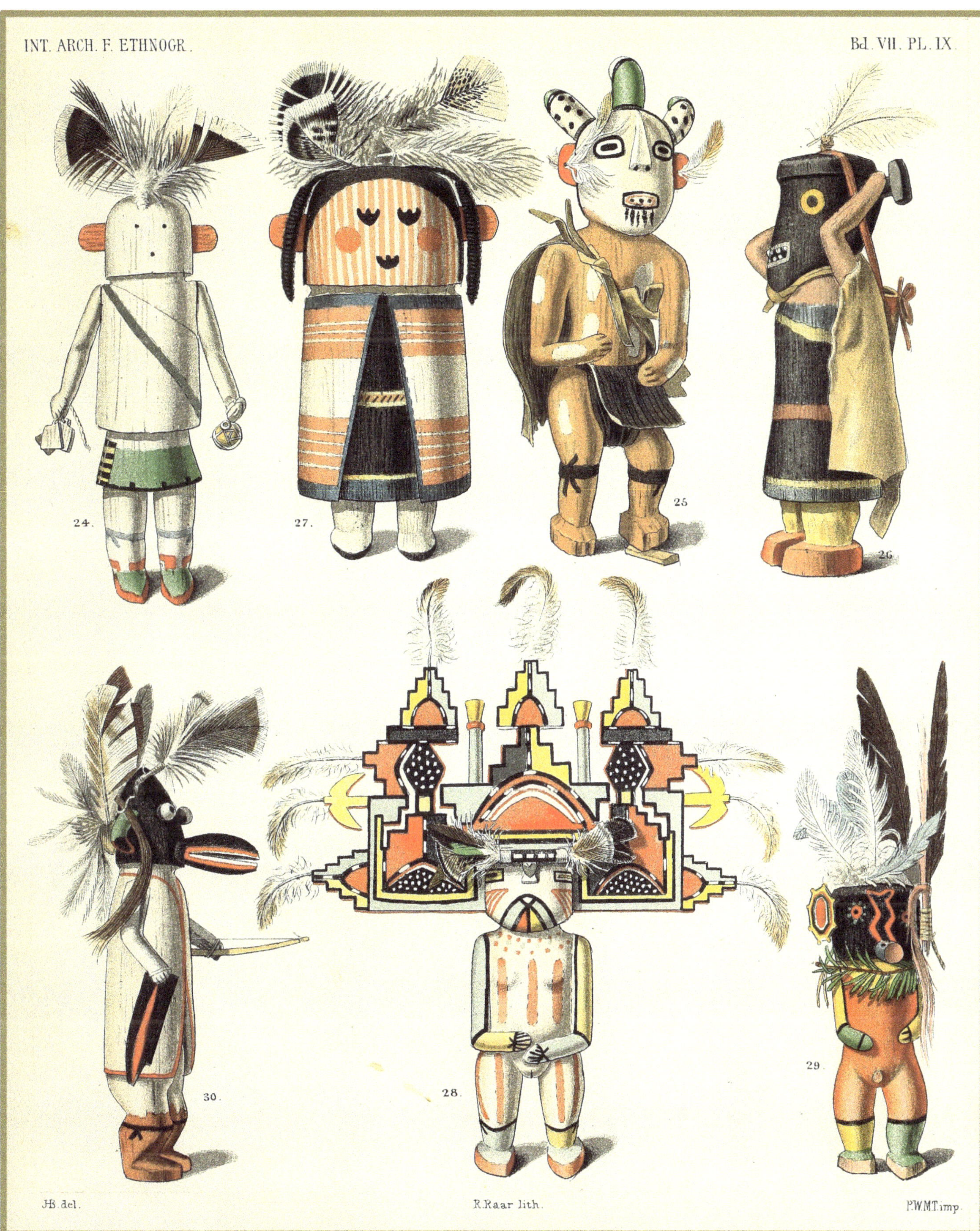

J.B. del. R. Raar lith. P.W.M.T. imp.

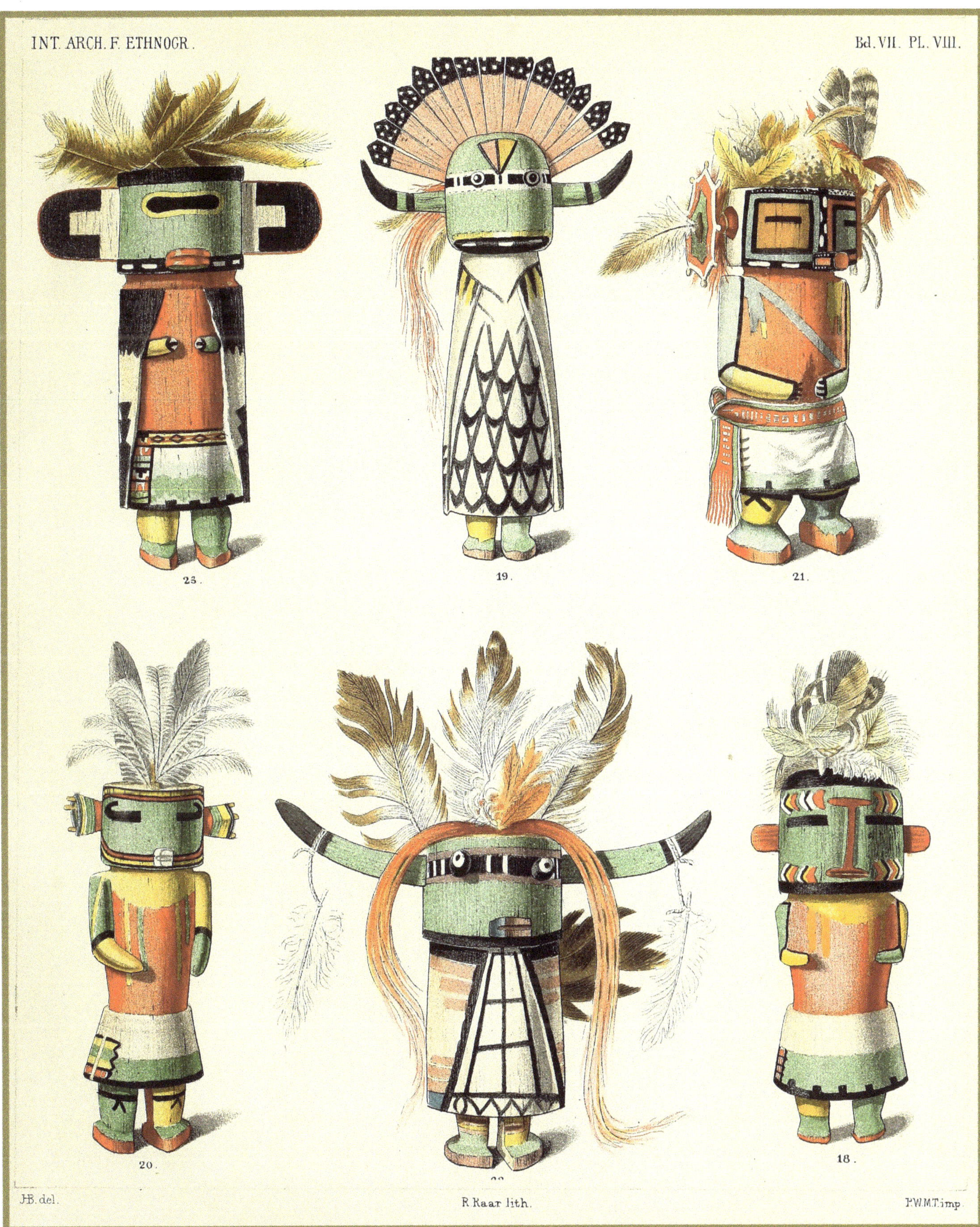
INT. ARCH. F. ETHNOGR.
Bd. VII. PL. VIII.
23.
19.
21.
20.
18.
J-B. del.
R. Raar lith.
P.W.M.T. imp.

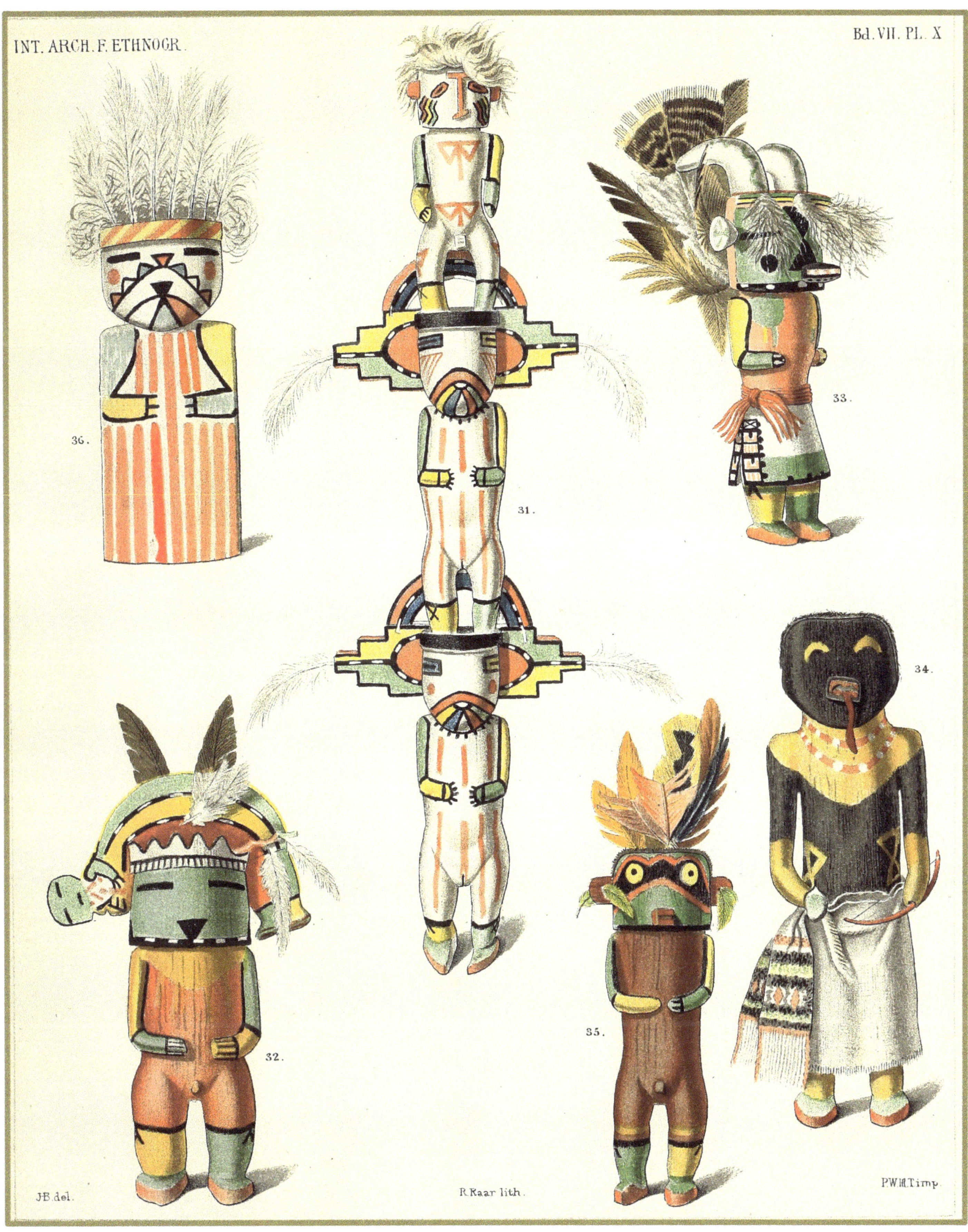
INT. ARCH. F. ETHNOGR.
Bd. VII. PL. X
36.
31.
33.
34.
32.
35.
J.B. del.
R. Kaar lith.
P.W.M. Trap. imp.

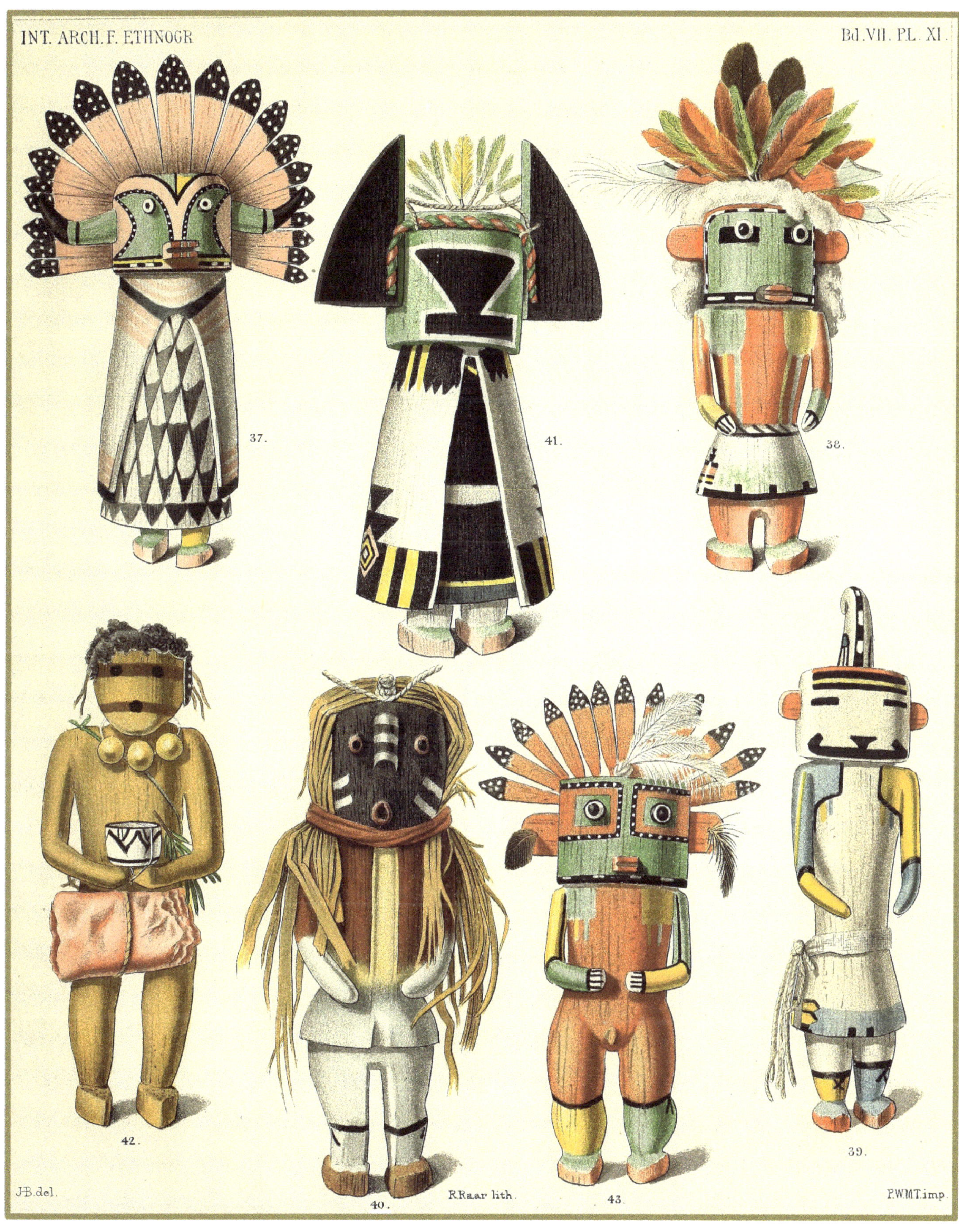

J.B. del. R. Raar lith. P.W.M.T. imp.

www.ingramcontent.com/pod-product-compliance
Lightning Source LLC
LaVergne TN
LVHW060621110826
845147LV00019B/1064
9781473330344